The
Amazing
Newborn

Overleaf: The baby girl in
the photograph is twenty-five
seconds old.

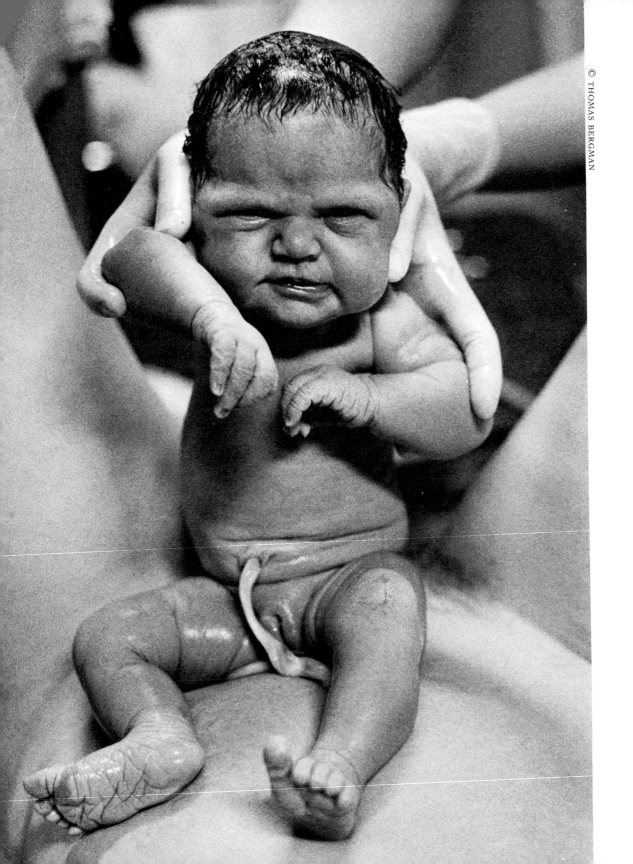

The Amazing Newborn

Marshall H. Klaus, M.D.
Phyllis H. Klaus, M.Ed., C.S.W.

A Merloyd Lawrence Book

✦ ADDISON-WESLEY PUBLISHING COMPANY

Reading, Massachusetts • Menlo Park, California • New York
Don Mills, Ontario • Wokingham, England • Amsterdam • Bonn
Sidney • Singapore • Tokyo • Madrid • San Juan • Paris
Seoul • Milan • Mexico City • Taipei

All photographs, unless otherwise identified, are from the films *The Amazing Newborn*, produced by Maureen Hack, M.D., and *The Ties That Bind*, produced by Patricia E. Rambasek, and reproduced courtesy of Case Western Reserve University. These photographs may not be reproduced or otherwise used for any purpose without prior written authorization from Case Western Reserve University.

The photographs on pages 9, 30, and 103 are reproduced by permission from *Maternal-Infant Bonding* by Marshall H. Klaus and John H. Kennell, copyright © 1976 by the C. V. Mosby Company, St. Louis, Missouri.

The photographs on page 86 are reproduced by permission from "Imitation of facial and manual gestures by human neonates" by A. N. Meltzoff and M. K. Moore, *Science* 198:75–78, October 1977.

The photographs on pages 90–91 are reproduced by permission from "Discrimination and imitation of facial expressions by neonates" by T. M. Field et al., *Science* 218: 179–181, October 1982.

The drawing on page 59 is reproduced by permission from "Intermodal matching by human neonates" by A. N. Meltzoff and R. W. Borton, *Nature* 282:403–404, copyright © by Macmillan Journals Ltd.

The photograph on page 102 is reproduced by permission from "Care of the mother of the high-risk infant" by Marshall H. Klaus and John H. Kennell, *Clinical Obstetrics and Gynecology* 14:926–954, September 1971.

The ultrasound images in Chapter 7 are reprinted by permission from "Ultrasound images of human fetal development" by Jason Birnholz and Elaine Farrel, *American Scientist* 72:608–614, 1984.

All drawings in Chapter 7 are by Laura Klaus.

Library of Congress Cataloging-in-Publication Data
Klaus, Marshall H.
    The amazing newborn.

    "A Merloyd Lawrence book."
    Includes index.
    1. Infant psychology. I. Klaus, Phyllis.
II. Title.
BF719.K53 1985   155.4'22   85-9048
ISBN 0-201-11672-3

Cover and chapter opener photographs © Mimi Cotter
Cover and interior design by Janis Capone
Set in 13-point Cochin by DEKR Corporation, Woburn, MA
ISBN 0-201-11672-3
8 9 10 11 12–MU–96959493
Eighth printing, May 1993

In loving appreciation to Susan, David, and Laura; Alisa, Laura, Sarah, John, Jocelyn, and Geoffrey—all wonderful children from whom we have learned so much, and to our grandson, Michael.

Contents

•

Preface

.

  This book came about in large part because of our delight in young infants. It is a book for baby watchers. Like bird-watchers, those who take time to observe newborn babies are often rewarded with startling sights and experiences.

  We are especially fortunate to be at work during a period when research into infancy is flowering all over the country. In addition, having a ready access to new babies has allowed us to explore personally not only our own observations but those made by many other students of newborn behavior. In this book we have attempted to illustrate each of the special and often newly discovered capacities with which human beings begin life. We have also, in Chapter 7, traced the origin of these capacities in the months before birth, an area of research that has opened up only since the advent of ultrasound.

  All the photographs in this book are of babies under ten days old. The photographs were collected from baby aficionados who spent long hours and days waiting for just the right second to photograph. As an example, the Swedish photographer Thomas Bergman spent three months on a labor and delivery floor and published forty-two photographs of his observations there. We are most fortunate to be able to include several pictures from his rare collection. Many of the other photos here are drawn from our film *The Amazing Newborn*, which is now shown in maternity hospitals, medical and nursing schools, and to childbirth education groups around the country.

One word of caution. As you read the text and view the pictures, remember that each infant is an individual with his or her own rhythm and style of responding. Moreover, babies have minds of their own and may not want to carry out on demand the antics described and pictured. As you enjoy your baby during this early period, you are likely to glimpse for a few moments many of the actions, responses, and abilities presented. You may even note some that are not described. Do not expect your baby, however, to display for your immediate viewing all the abilities illustrated. As our book points out, certain responses occur only when the newborn is in a particular state of alertness.

When our own children were born, we were not aware of all their amazing talents and abilities. At that time, most everyone—including doctors—believed not only that infants could not see or focus their eyes, but also that they certainly would not respond to or recognize their mother's voice. No one talked about the possibility that an infant could imitate facial expressions, respond to rhythms of language, reach for objects, and start to learn at such an early age.

As we gradually recognized the presence of finely tuned senses from the moment of birth, we began to reflect on the environment that greets the newborn. We were forced to question the appropriateness of brightly lit, noisy newborn nurseries in the hope of changing hospital practice. Wouldn't a responsive and sensitive baby be happier with his or her mother most of the day, with someone entirely devoted to understanding this particular baby's needs and responses? Fortunately, many hospitals now encourage early interaction, a quiet environment for the new family, and even rooming-in at least part of every day. We hope that nurses and all others involved in childbirth and newborn care will find the information in this book helpful as they continue to adapt their caregiving practices to what is now known about the needs of the human infant.

Many of our early insights into newborn behavior resulted from talking with Dr. Robert Fantz of Cleveland about his pioneering observations of infant vision. Also especially meaningful have been discussions with T. Berry Brazelton, Joseph Fagan, Simone Miranda, Tiffany Field, Louis Sander, Andrew Meltzoff, Anneliese Korner, Aidan Macfarlane, Colin Trevarthen, Steven Robertson, Robert Emde, Anthony DeCasper, Claudine Amiel-Tison, Dan Stern, Jason Birnholz, Kathryn Barnard, Ruth Merkatz, and James and Joyce Robertson. Close collaboration with our long-term colleague John Kennell has been invaluable in furthering our understanding of this area. The skill and patience of the creative filmmaker Patricia Rambasek, who persevered in making the film *The Amazing Newborn,* even though she initially did not believe that babies could do all these things, deserve special credit. And of course, thanks to our associate Maureen Hack, whose knowledge and perception made the film possible. We owe much appreciation to the skill and talents of our editor, Merloyd Lawrence. Thanks also to Judy Copeman for her excellent manuscript typing.

Our greatest debt is to the parents of the newborns that we studied and to the babies themselves, a constant source of inspiration, delight, and pure pleasure. We hope that the parents of all future generations will enjoy their infants a bit more because of this book.

Marshall H. Klaus, M.D.
Phyllis H. Klaus, M.Ed., C.S.W.

1
·

Waking
to the
World

·

The baby on the opposite page is only six minutes old. Something very special occurs within the first hour after birth. If the environment is quiet, the birthing without complications, the lights lowered, the handling diminished, newborn infants—aside from all the physiological adaptations they must make—begin in a uniquely human way to adapt to the new experience of being in the world.

This infant girl, only six minutes old, is in what is known as the quiet alert state of consciousness.

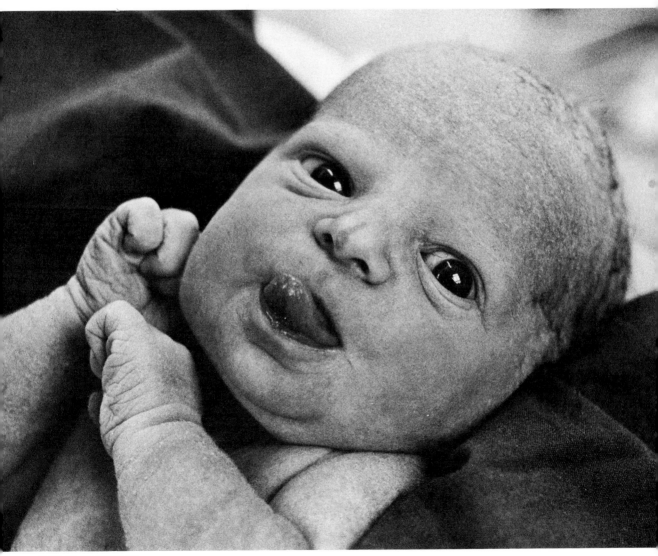

3

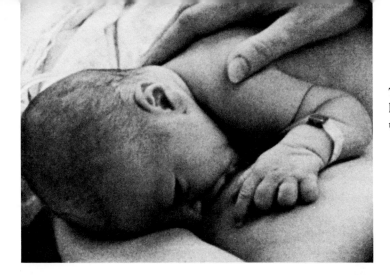

This nursing newborn boy, less than one hour old, is getting to know his mother.

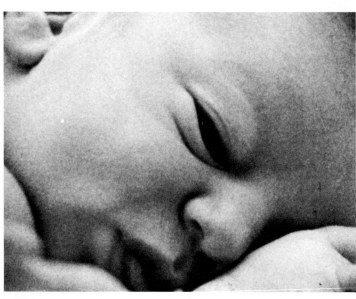

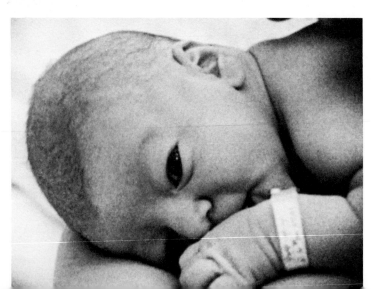

One of the newborn's first responses is to move into a quiet but alert state of consciousness. The baby is still; his body molds to yours; his hands touch your skin; his eyes open wide and are bright and shiny. He looks directly at you.

This special alert state, this innate ability to communicate, may be the initial preparation for becoming attached to other human beings. One feels awed by the intensity and appealing power of this little bud of humanity meeting the world for the first time.

Dressed for the first time, this hour-old boy stares intently at the photographer.

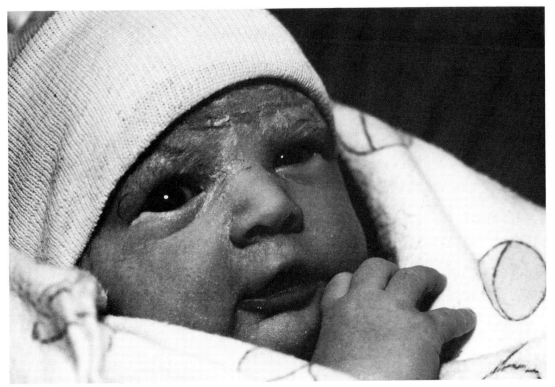

ALEXANDRA DANE DOR-NER

It was not until the mid-1960s that physicians and psychologists believed that the newborn infant's brain was developed to anything more than a primitive level. At birth the infant was considered a somewhat limited creature, capable of performing only the simple functions of eating, moving, sleeping, and crying. In spite of the fact that many mothers were convinced that their babies could see and respond to them, newborns were then described as existing in a world William James portrayed as "blooming, buzzing confusion."

The revolution in our understanding of the amazing abilities of newborns began with the work of two very perceptive scientists who scrutinized the marvelous organization and levels of newborn behavior. Dr. Peter Wolff, a child psychiatrist in Boston, worked in homes with newborn babies. He sat for long periods, unobtrusively recording their every action, awake and asleep. Independently, Dr. Heinz Prechtl made similar studies in Groningen, Holland, but added recordings of heart rate, breathing, and brain waves. These researchers documented every aspect of newborn behavior: grimaces, hiccups, sneezes, tremors, and twitches. They noted arm and leg motion as well as breathing and sucking activity. They recorded minute eye and eyelid movements. In short, they documented any and all reflexes and responses to the environment.

Having gathered detailed descriptions over many days and from many newborns, both Drs. Wolff and Prechtl then arranged their information in creative ways that led to key discoveries. They found that seemingly random and unrelated activities actually fell into behavioral groups that made surprising sense. They classified these patterns into six different states of consciousness according to the infant's degree of wakefulness or sleep. By closely observing your own baby, you will soon learn to recognize the two sleep states, quiet sleep and active sleep; as well as the three awake states— quiet alert, active alert, and crying. The other state, drowsiness, is a transition between sleep and wakefulness.

Each of these six states is accompanied by quite specific and individual behaviors. We do not understand how the brain produces the distinctions, but we do recognize that for the human infant there are six ways of being or acting in the world. One can liken these states of consciousness to the changing of sets for acts in a play. Each act has its own setting, time, and mood, and the action makes sense only with the appropriate scenery. Likewise, for the newborn, each state of consciousness has a specific set of behaviors.

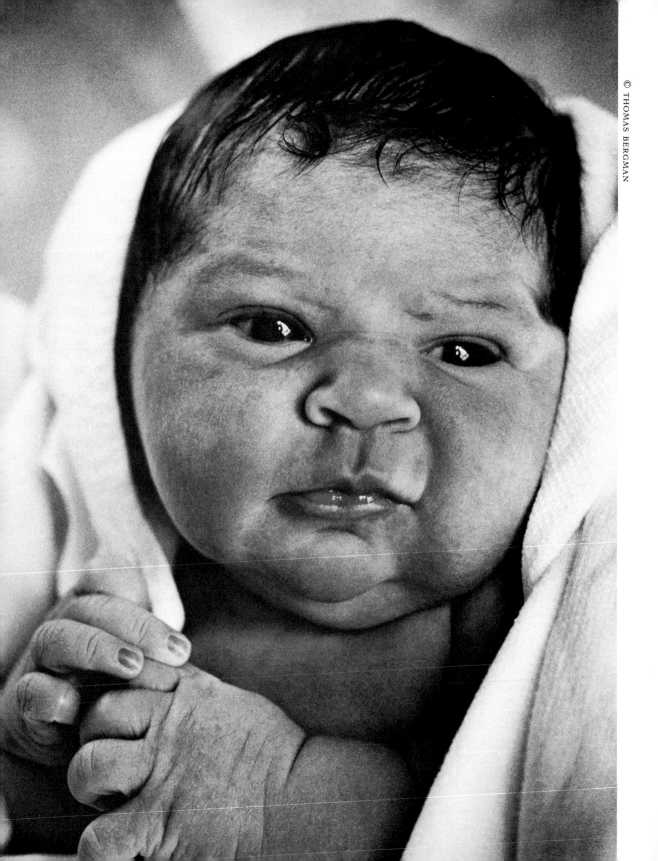

This newborn in the quiet alert state is only eleven minutes old.

In the quiet alert state, which is very similar to the conscious attention we see in our friends when they are listening closely to us, babies rarely move. Their eyes are wide open, bright and shiny. In this state, newborns are especially fun to play with. They can follow a red ball, select pictures, and even imitate their mother's face.

Right after birth, within the first hour of life, normal infants have a prolonged period of quiet alertness, averaging forty minutes, during which they look directly at their mother's and father's face and eyes and can respond to voices. It is as though newborns had rehearsed the perfect approach to the first meeting with their parents. (This may in fact be so; sleeping and waking states begin long before birth, as we will see in Chapter 7.) In this state, motor activity is suppressed and all the baby's energy seems to be channeled into seeing and hearing.

A brand-new baby giving all his attention to his mother

Michael and his mother enjoying each other

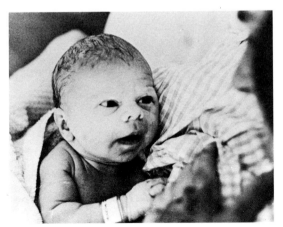

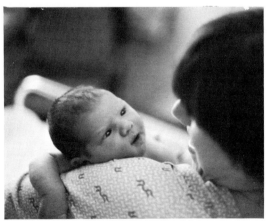

C. V. MOSBY CO.

DAVID KLAUS

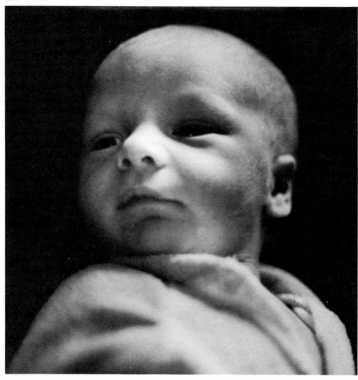

Newborn curiosity

During the first week of life, the normal baby spends about 10 percent of any twenty-four-hour day in this exciting and receptive state. Such alertness allows newborns to take in much of their surroundings and to respond and adapt to the environment. When your baby is in this state, you will see the first evidence of natural curiosity as the infant searches to understand the world.

During the active alert state, your baby is very different. There is frequent movement, the eyes look about, and the baby makes small sounds. This state appears before eating or when babies are fussy. Observations have shown that although the baby does not move continuously, there are episodes of movement that occur with a special rhythm. About every one to two minutes, your baby will move his arms, legs, body, or face. These movements may serve an adaptive purpose. Some scientists believe that they convey clues to parents about what their baby needs. Others believe that because these movements are interesting to watch, they may promote a natural interaction between parents and babies. Similar bursts of movements, which may be regulated by some sort of internal clock within the baby's brain, have even been detected in the fetus as well by placing sensitive measuring devices on the mother's abdomen late in pregnancy.

Jenny in the active alert state

WRIGHT WILLIAMSON

The crying state, which is one obvious way for infants to communicate, occurs when the baby is hungry or uncomfortable. An infant's eyes may be open or tightly closed when crying, the face is

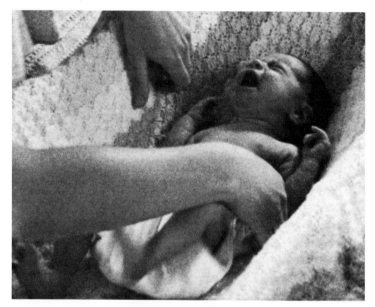

Leah crying

A few seconds later, Leah immediately becomes quiet when placed on her mother's shoulder.

By raising Leah to her shoulder, this mother has changed her baby's state from crying to quiet alert. Now Leah and her father gaze at each other.

contorted and red, and the arms and legs move vigorously. Many mothers know that they can change babies' crying states by picking them up, soothing them, and putting them to the shoulder as shown here. The mothers who pick up their crying infants are giving them an opportunity not only to be quietly awake but also to learn about their world by scanning the room. Originally researchers thought it was the upright position that soothed the baby. However, it turns out that it is the movement toward that position rather than the position itself that changes the baby into the quiet alert state.

The state called drowsiness usually occurs while the baby is waking up or falling asleep. The baby may continue to move, sometimes smiling, frowning, or pursing the lips. The eyes have a dull glazed appearance and usually do not focus. The lids are droopy, and, just before closing, the eyes may roll upward.

Just before sleep

Leah slips into the state called drowsiness.

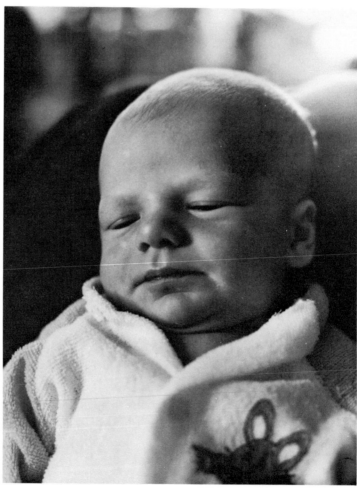

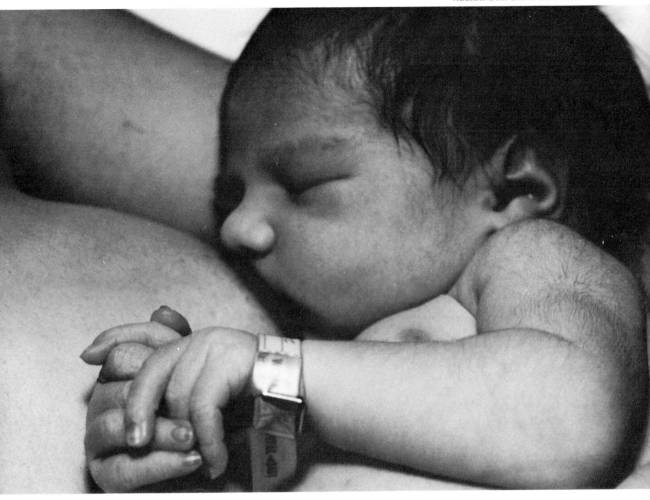

Newborn asleep at his mother's breast

During the newborn period, an infant sleeps most of the time—about 90 percent of the day or night—and often will fall asleep right at the breast. Half of this sleep time is spent in quiet sleep, the other half in active sleep. These two states alternate about every thirty minutes during sleep.

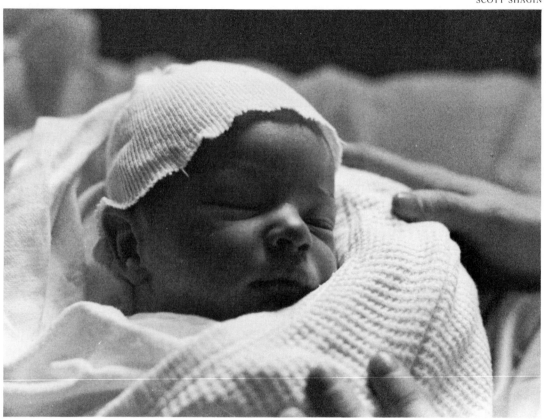

**The serenity of newborn
sleep**

In quiet sleep, your baby's face is relaxed and the eyelids are closed and still. There are no body movements except rare startles and very, very fine mouth movements. In this state, infants are at full rest and breathing is very regular because they take in the same amount of air with each breath.

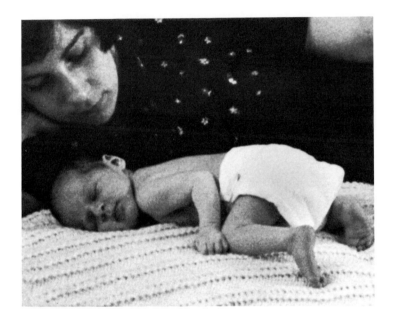

Leah in what is known as quiet, or deep, sleep

In active sleep, an infant's eyes are usually closed, but occasionally they will flutter from closed to open. One can often see the eyes move under the lids. Dr. Jason Birnholz of Rush Medical College of Chicago has observed the eye motion or stillness accompanying these two states in the womb by means of ultrasound (see Chapter 7). The term "rapid eye movement" or REM sleep originated from the eye movements observed during this type of restless sleep. In active sleep, you will notice occasional body activity that ranges from movement of the baby's arms and legs to stirring of the entire body. Breathing is not regular and is slightly faster than in quiet sleep. While they remain asleep, infants in this state often make funny faces—grimaces, smiles, frowns—and may display chewing movements or bursts of sucking. When babies wake, they usually have been in active rather than quiet sleep. Adults experience such REM sleep when they are dreaming; no one knows whether infants also are dreaming in this particular sleep state.

Notice the extent of movement during active sleep.

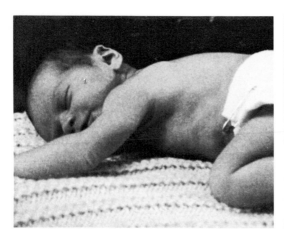
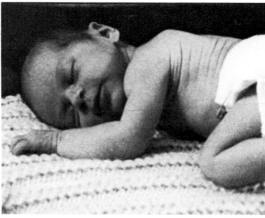

Mouth and eye movements in active sleep, also called dream or rapid eye movement (REM) sleep

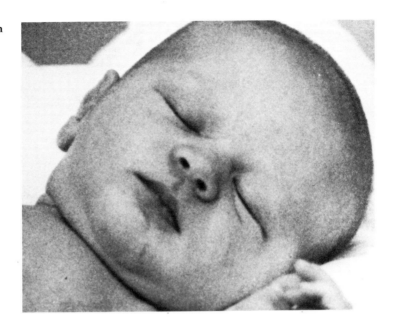

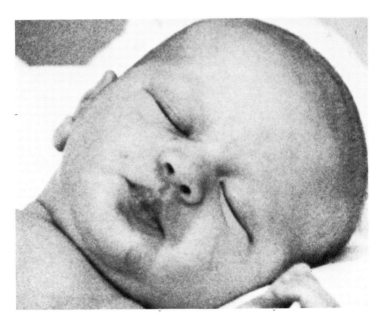

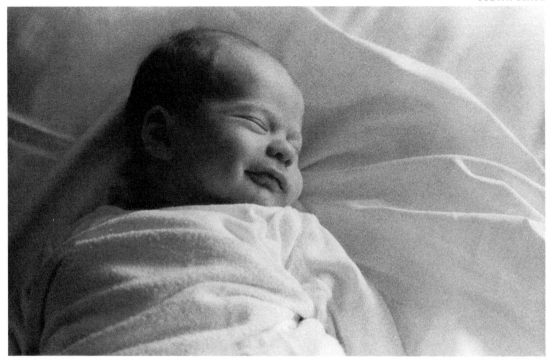

By recognizing the different states and re-
alizing when they occur and what the expected
responses are in each, parents not only can get to
know their infants but also can provide most sen-
sitively for their needs. For instance, when a baby
is whimpering slightly and is stirring in active sleep,
a parent who is aware that this occurs in thirty-
minutes cycles will not rush to feed or change the
baby unless this gentle activity turns into the active
awake and then crying states.

With their brilliant observations, Drs.
Prechtl and Wolff have allowed us to perceive order in what formerly seemed to be random behavior. Once we understand and recognize the six
patterns of newborn behavior, the mysterious,
shifting world of these new humans begins to make
much more sense.

A pleasant dream?

2
·
What Does the Newborn See?
·

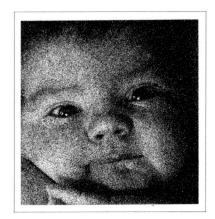

The amazing capacity for responsiveness already present in the newborn in the first minutes, hours, and days of life is especially apparent in the infant's ability to see. For years mothers have been saying that soon after birth their baby could see and respond visually to them. Doctors were reluctant to believe them. However, it is now evident that the mothers were right.

A mother learning about her two-hour-old baby, as the baby surveys the world

© THOMAS BERGMAN

In 1960 a very creative psychologist, Dr. Robert Fantz, conducted the first research that confirmed the newborn infant's ability to see. Applying a method for documenting vision that he had used with chickens and monkeys, Dr. Fantz adapted his research to human infants. It was only after these studies of newborn visual fixation that psychologists and the medical profession began to accept the fact that the infant could see, even at birth. The apparatus he used is shown here.

Dr. Fantz about to study a baby's sight

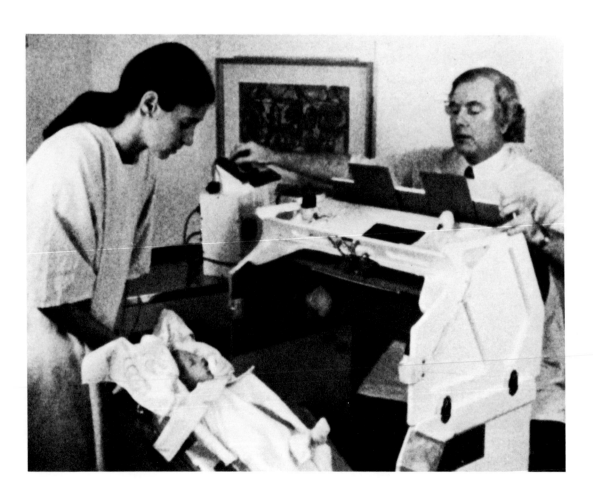

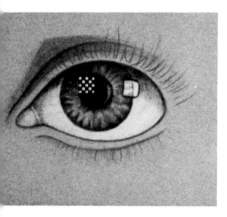

This is an illustration of what Dr. Fantz might see on the surface of the eye. The infant is looking at the checkerboard pattern, not the white square, since the checkerboard is directly over the pupil.

Dr. Fantz's procedure is based on the fact that a picture that is being looked at, or "fixated," is reflected from the cornea of the eye over the pupil. When the reflection of the picture is seen on the surface of the pupil (the black portion within the center of the eye), the picture is aligned in such a way that it falls on the center of the retina (a recording device within the eye that relays the visual image to the brain).

A quiet awake baby is placed in an adjustable seat under a hood where he is shown two pictures. A peephole between the two pictures enables an observer to discover easily what the baby is looking at by watching the baby's pupils.

In the illustration of the eye above, two patterns—a checkerboard and a plain white square—are reflected on the surface of the eye. Since the checkerboard is directly over the pupil

In the chamber, the infant is shown two patterns.

Dr. Fantz looks at the infant's eyes through a small peephole.

of the eye, it is the pattern being looked at. To be sure that the infant is truly interested and is not looking at the picture by chance, the pictures are reversed every ten seconds, and each time the observer checks and records which pattern is directly over the pupils.

By this method, Dr. Fantz demonstrated that the infant shows preferences even among abstract patterns and is especially attracted to sharp outlines as well as light and dark contrasts. If the pattern is dark, newborns are apt to search for light areas. If it is light, the opposite is true. And if they find contrasting edges or contours, their eyes will scan in such a way as to provide maximum stimulation to the retina. Both eyes actually look in the direction of the pattern and the baby shows attention not only by looking, but also by lifting the upper eyelid, by "brightening" the eye, and by ceasing to suck. Babies can also recognize color.

An abstract pattern is placed in the chamber for the infant's viewing.

The infant is looking at the abstract pattern since it can be seen reflected directly on his pupils.

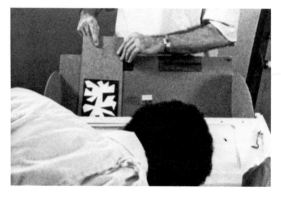

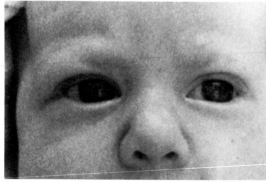

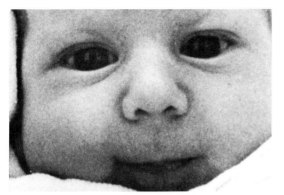 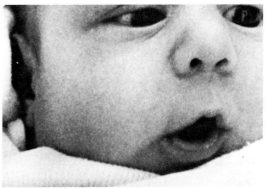

This baby is being shown the patterns noted on page 25, large and small squares. Since neither pattern is over the pupil, he is not looking specifically at the pattern, but straight ahead into the chamber.

Now the infant is looking at the large squares, which can be seen reflected directly in the center of his pupil.

In addition, Dr. Fantz discovered that the newborn has an innate ability to recognize patterns and to select certain forms for longer examination. The tendency to look longer or more often at a particular picture or pattern indicates the capabilities of distinguishing between objects or patterns and of expressing preferences. By patiently studying hundreds of babies, Dr. Fantz documented that the infants look longer at—or prefer—patterned (circles and strips) over plain surfaces. Further, they prefer complex patterns with more elements over simpler and less detailed patterns. He later showed that infants also prefer curving rather than straight patterns.

The possibility that these selections might indicate an adaptive preference for human faces is a fascinating issue currently being investigated. Do they recognize the human face or are they just attracted to the contrast of features—eyes, hair, facial outline—with the background? This dispute has been investigated by asking whether, given a choice, an infant prefers a scrambled or a regular face. In spite of subtle differences in several studies, it appears that the infant is especially attracted to the regular face.

What does the baby prefer, the regular or the scrambled face?

Other researchers noted that newborns are especially attracted to movement. When a moving object catches their attention, they are apt to focus on it. They will follow it with their eyes and sometimes with their heads as well. If a red ball is moved slowly at a distance of ten inches from their face, they will follow it first with their eyes and then turn their head horizontally and sometimes verti-

The infant is looking directly at the red ball.

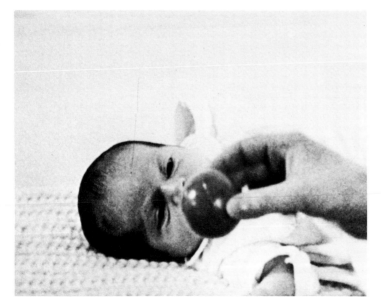

cally. Initially the babies' attention will be intense, but after a few minutes they lose some interest. They may turn away, and sometimes they become drowsy or actually fall asleep or "tune out" an apparently uninteresting image.

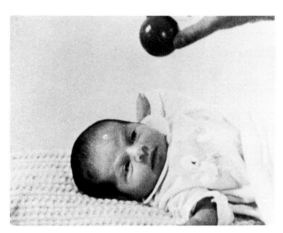

The red ball is moved and the infant begins to follow the ball,

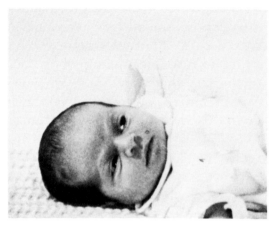

first with only her eyes.

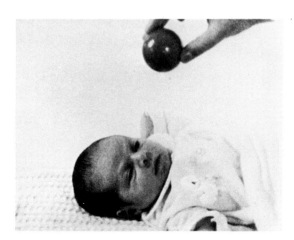

A short time later, she also begins to turn her head.

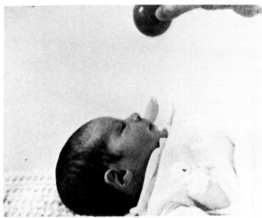

She continues to follow the ball.

In contrast other infants become "locked in" or "hooked" on what they are looking at and will stare at an object for periods of up to ten minutes. Such distinct differences between babies intrigue both researchers and parents.

This ability to see and focus on visual objects occurs mainly during the quiet alert state and thus can be missed by anyone not sensitive to the baby's cues. Another reason for our previous inability to recognize that newborns can see is related to the fact that they are born nearsighted and so cannot initially accommodate their vision to distances. Newborn vision is best in a range of eight to ten inches from the face. It is not surprising to realize that this is about the same distance from which an infant views his mother's face during a feeding. If objects are moved too close or too far, they go out of focus and can be seen only as a haze or blur. If you want to test your infant's ability to focus and follow, objects should be kept in that eight-to-ten-inch range. Make sure that you have your baby's attention (the baby should be looking directly at the object) before you begin to move the object slowly.

Something has caught Ben's attention.

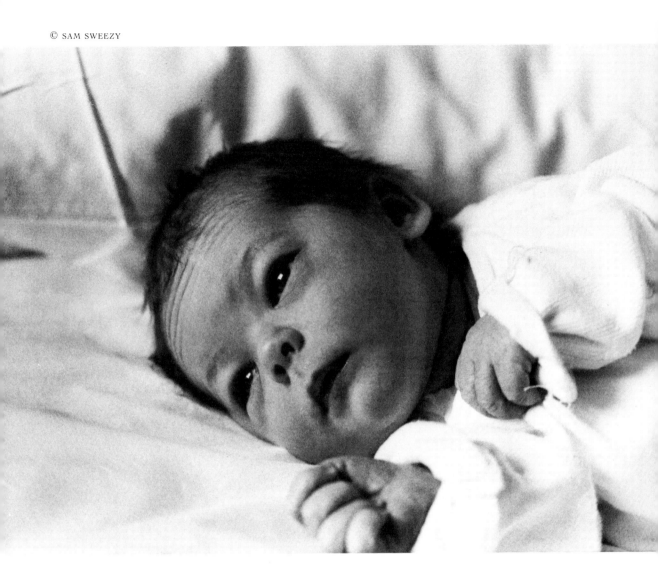

This two-day-old baby is intrigued by a bright light.

Using an infrared camera, doctors have discovered that newborns tend to scan the outer contours of patterns rather than look at inner details. Similarly, when babies look at human faces, they usually scan the outline and then move to the eyes and mouth. Eyes are particularly engrossing to the infant. In the sequence shown here, Leah, just a few hours old, scans her mother's face and then reaches to touch what she is looking at (an unusual example of the coordination of touch and vision).

Leah begins to follow the
outline of her mother's face.

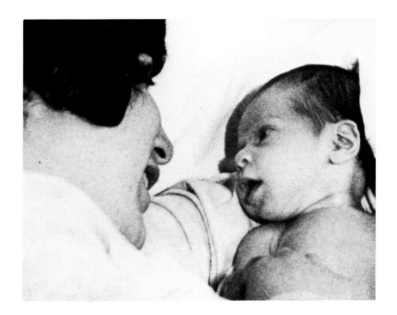

Leah now looks at the mouth
and lifts her hand.

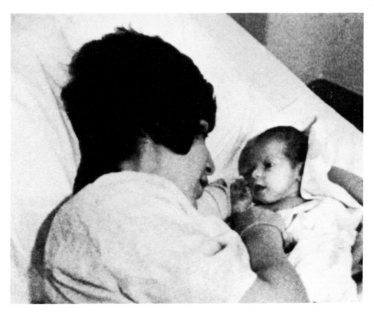

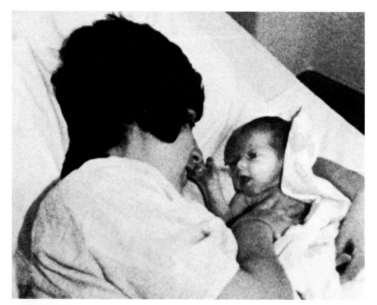

Here Leah reaches to touch what she sees.

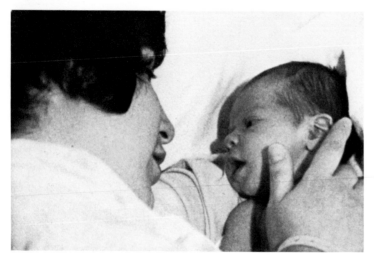

Leah looks at her mother's face.

Leah's mother responds.

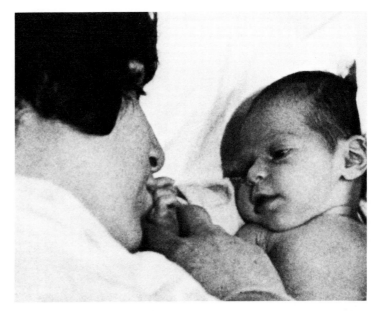

Leah is tired and turns away.

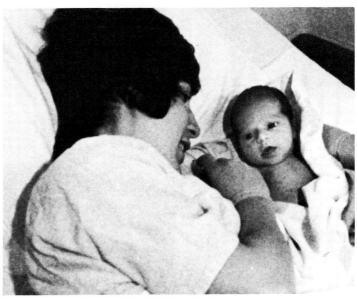

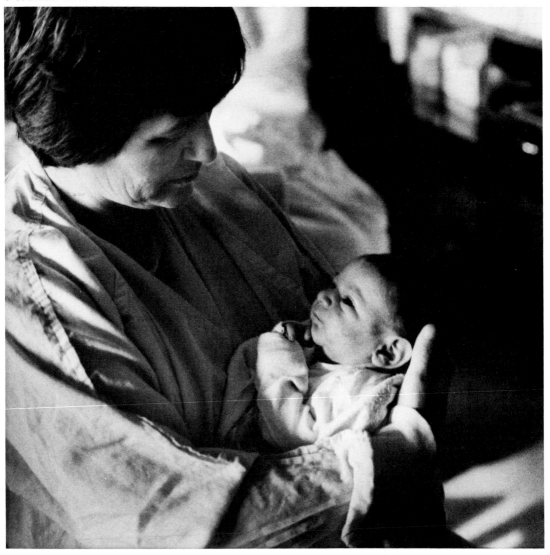

A Mexican mother and infant gaze at each other in the first minutes of the baby's life.

In the quiet alert state, as the eyes become bright and widely open, the infant will often stop moving or sucking and become very still. These short periods of rapt visual attention, occurring shortly after birth and throughout this early period, draw the newborn into eye-to-eye contact, a vital element in human interaction. In this mutual gaze, the first dialogue begins; both parent and child seem magnetically drawn into communication.

Interesting visual objects can change an infant's state of consciousness. A drowsy or crying baby can become quietly alert if something fascinating catches his eye. The state of quiet alertness can sometimes be increased or maintained by changing what a baby is able to see from his bassinet or crib.

Up to now, the discussion has centered on only what an infant sees. Newborns are also capable of processing visual information, remembering what they have seen, and using that information. If infants are shown the same picture for a long period of time, they tend to decrease their looking time, as if bored. However, if shown a new and different picture, they demonstrate renewed interest. This is called "response to novelty" and may signify an early ability to remember a picture already seen. It has also been shown that if you put a mask on a mother's face when her infant is eight days old, her infant will recognize the change and look at her frequently during feedings as if something is wrong or different. This same infant will take less milk and when placed down to nap will be restless and will not fall asleep quickly. The baby will also sleep for a shorter period of time than previously. This evidence suggests that newborns can recognize their mothers and actually remember their faces. As an example, a mother of a one-day-old baby noticed that her baby appeared quite puzzled when she took off her contact lenses and put on her horn-rimmed glasses. Such feats of visual perception and memory by the baby indicate that the infant's visual talent is based not only on reflex eye movement but on higher brain function as well.

KIP KOZLOWSKI

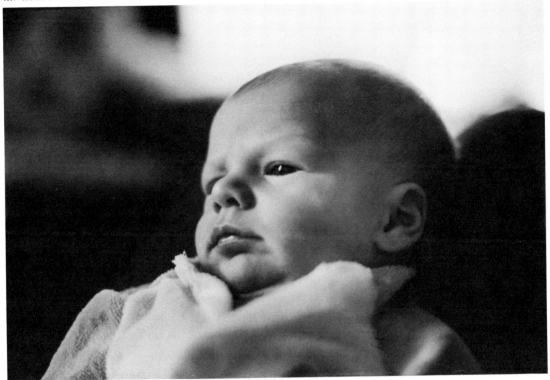

**Visual concentration in a
newborn boy**

Infants are active in their visual responses. When alert, babies not only can see, they look about spontaneously. They can even recognize depth and may respond with a defensive reaction to approaching objects. And, as already noted, they are selective—they prefer complexity, diversity, and movement—and they have visual memory.

The fact that parents' faces are of special interest to the infant also helps draw the parents to the infant. The newborn's visual curiosity and ability to have eye-to-eye contact is, of course, very rewarding for parents and caretakers. Because infants blink less than adults, they have a wondrous staring sort of gaze or look. Along with other infant facial features, such as prominent forehead and chubby cheeks, these large inquiring eyes are especially appealing. Just as babies seem born with a preference for human faces, adults may be programmed to enjoy and be drawn to small babies.

One of the primary nonverbal ways in which humans communicate is by looking at one another. A baby's early visual ability and parents' insatiable desire to admire their baby create endless opportunities to experience, discover, and interact with one another.

3
·

Hearing,
Touch,
Taste,
and Smell
·

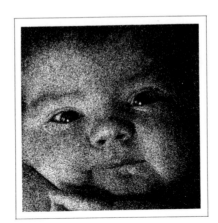

Months before birth, babies' ability *to hear* is already acute and well developed. They can distinguish between types of sound (for example, a buzzer or a bell), loudness and pitch, different voices, familiar and unfamiliar sounds, and they can even determine the direction from which sound is coming.

Newborn babies prefer high-pitched voices, and mothers and fathers seem instinctively to use high-pitched voices when they first talk to their babies after delivery. Such "baby talk" seems to be a universal phenomenon. Charles A. Ferguson, a linguist at Stanford, has shown that mothers of six different nationalities break into similar sounds and nonsense syllables, using short sentences and falsetto voices, whatever their native language.

Infants respond to inanimate sounds as well. When a small bell is rung, they will orient to the sound by first turning their eyes and then their head in the direction of the sound. Orienting to sound is something humans do without thinking. Our heads are like antennae moving automatically into position for the best reception. Newborns start to do this from the first moments after birth; they look to the right when the sound is coming from the right and to the left when the sound is from the left. The nerves connecting vision and hearing are already developed in the newborn.

When first hearing the bell, Leah moves her eyes in the direction of the sound.

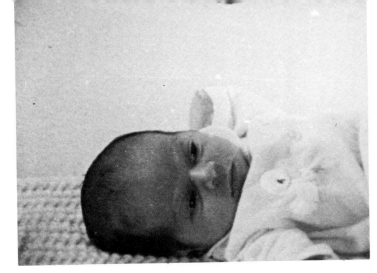

Leah then begins to follow with her head.

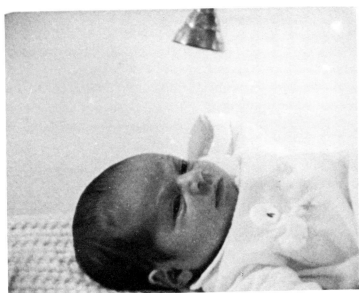

Finally, she moves her head so she can see what she hears.

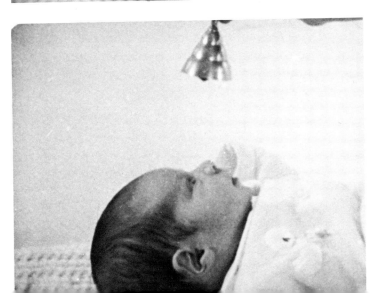

This ability to look toward the source of the sound may be part of the infant's attempt to get better reception, or perhaps this eye-and-ear response may be one of the many built-in connections between two or more senses—an adaptive response that ensures experiencing the environment as fully as possible.

Research has shown that babies not only can make associations between sound and other senses, but also can be taught to respond in different ways to the same sound and, if permitted, will exert some control in choosing sounds they want to hear. For instance, one-day-old infants have mastered the following complex experiment. They learned to turn their head to the right at the sound of a bell; but they also learned *not* to turn their head to the right at the sound of a buzzer. This was achieved by rewarding them with sugar water only when they responded to the bell. Then they were taught the reverse, learning it very quickly. That is, they turned their head to the right only for the buzzer, but not for the bell, this time being rewarded with sugar water only when the buzzer sounded. This ability to make associations from different sensory input at an early age may represent a fundamental process of human learning.

Researchers have also asked whether infants could coordinate the hand and the ear in the same way they coordinate the hand and the eye. Could they reach for objects using the sense of sound instead of relying only on sight as a guide to locate something? They surmised that because infants are generally passive recipients of sound and cannot turn away from sounds in the environment as one would turn away from sights (close the eyes), they may not develop or use the sensory connection between hearing and touch. Since babies exert no active control over what they hear, they might lose interest, become habituated, or lose the motivation or the need to use this skill.

T. G. R. Bower at the University of Edinburgh designed a device that would give infants control over the sounds they heard. He used earphones with ultrasonic receivers that transmitted different audible sounds to the infant depending on the position of the baby's head in relationship to different objects. One study with a blind infant illustrated that the infant could detect an object in front of him when the sonic device indicated that the object was present. The infant raised his hands as if he had "seen" the object. These different perceptual skills are present at birth and continue to evolve and develop with time. The newborn has a flexible variety of ways to perceive his world.

A mother engages her son with her voice and face.

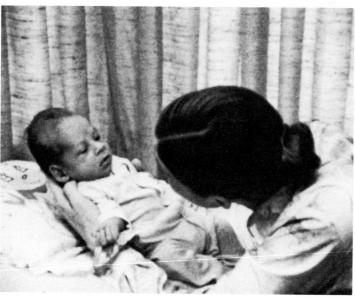

As she continues to talk, he follows her voice and face.

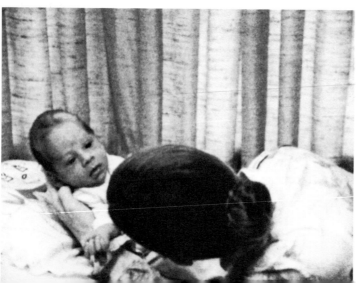

The baby turns his head and eyes far to the right, continuing to follow his mother's voice and face.

Infants are most responsive to human voices. You can have fun with your baby when he is in a quiet alert state by talking a short distance from one ear in a high-pitched voice. You may first notice your baby's eyes turning in the direction of your voice, and almost simultaneously, the baby's head will turn, his face brighten, and his eyes open a bit wider. Even more appealing to the infant is being talked to and looked at simultaneously.

This baby boy turns far to the right to look at a woman talking to him in a high-pitched voice.

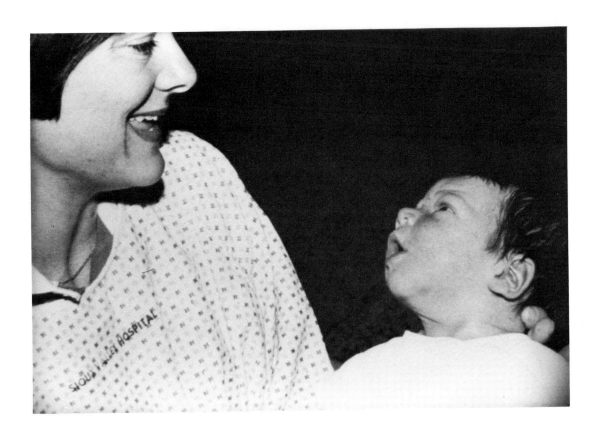

This baby girl is entranced by what she sees and hears.

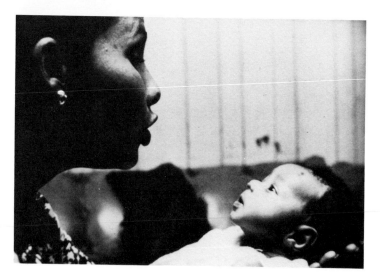

She almost appears to be imitating her mother.

Discovering what human infants prefer to listen to has required considerable ingenuity. Dr. Anthony DeCasper at the University of North Carolina recognized that since infants have superb innate control of their mouths and lips, they might be able to indicate a preference by changing their sucking rate or tempo. He therefore contrived the following experiment. Working with one- to two-day-old infants in the alert state, Dr. DeCasper placed a nipple in the mouth of each baby and fitted the baby with a pair of padded earphones. The nipple was attached to a device that triggered different recordings. For example, if the infant sucked at a high rate, she would hear a recording of a woman's voice, and when she sucked at a low rate, she would hear a man's recorded voice.

Dr. DeCasper placed padded earphones on this day-old infant and arranged for her to control what she heard by changing her sucking rate.

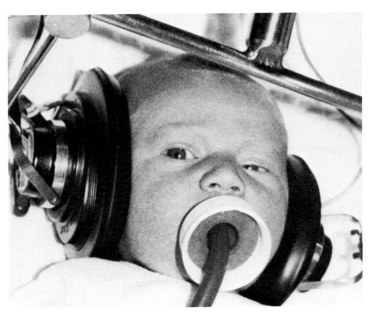

ANTHONY DECASPER/WALTER SALINGER

Eleven out of twelve babies tested in this manner sucked at the high rate to hear the woman's voice. To be sure that this was not just related to preferring to suck at a high rate, the woman's high-pitched voice was alternated so that for some of the babies it was heard when they sucked at a low rate. Almost all infants quickly learned that their sucking rate determined what they heard. Here were one- and two-day-old babies controlling their environment—just as adults control part of their environment when they turn on Mozart instead of rock music. The unusually creative aspect of this study was linking the control of what the babies heard to something that they could accurately or precisely direct (sucking). Using similar techniques, Dr. DeCasper found that infants prefer their mother's voice over other women's voices but, in the immediate newborn period, do not prefer their father's voice to that of another male. Recognition of their father's voice comes slightly later. Their preference for their mother's voice may be the enduring result of continually hearing their mother's voice during fetal life, or it might possibly be due to the fact that, at normal conversational levels, male voices are less easily distinguishable through the uterine wall because of their lower pitch.

A French obstetrician investigated prenatal hearing by placing a very small microphone into the uterus while mothers were in labor (after the membranes had broken) and recording the intensity of sound reaching the infant through the uterus. He also observed a variety of different responses (heart rate and movement, for example) that babies made to different types of sounds. Most sounds penetrated the uterine and abdominal wall.

In one such experiment, he could clearly hear the unmistakable sounds and levels of voices in the room, the mother's internal body sounds, and Beethoven's Ninth Symphony being played in the delivery suite!

Many people have wondered if this capacity to pick up and respond to sound during fetal life might influence musical preferences or ability, as well as account for the infant's response and familiarity to its mother's voice. After speaking with a talented thirteen-year-old cellist who has already appeared with major symphony orchestras and going back into her prenatal history, it was discovered that her mother was a practicing musician and during her pregnancy with this daughter had played the violin daily in a chamber music group. Many great composers had parents who were musicians. Of course the experience of early childhood could just as well be the key factor, not to mention lessons, hard work, and talent.

To learn if babies have any memory of what they hear in utero, Dr. DeCasper and his colleagues did another series of intriguing studies. They initially tape-recorded each of sixteen mothers while the women read both Dr. Seuss's *The Cat in the Hat* and a poem called *The King, the Mice and the Cheese*. During the last six and a half weeks of their pregnancy, each mother in the study was asked to read aloud only one of these children's stories to her fetus, which she did twice a day. Thus each fetus had a total of about five hours of listening time to the same story read over and over until birth. At three days of age, padded earphones were placed on the babies' ears and the recordings of both of these stories were played to them. The babies heard one story if they sucked rapidly and the other story if they sucked slowly. Amazingly, fifteen out of the sixteen newborns sucked at the right rate to receive the story that they had heard their mothers reading over and over again when they were fetuses—not too different from the requests of a toddler to hear again and again a favorite story!

When medical students are first introduced to newborn babies, they are always surprised at the alacrity of response the babies give their mother in comparison to a stranger. The babies become quiet at the sound of her voice and almost immediately begin to turn their head. It has been shown that infants are already coordinating sight, sound, and memory of their mother's voice within the first two weeks. It was fascinating to mothers in one study that their infants showed much confusion and distress when hearing the mother's voice apparently coming from another woman's face or seeing their mother's face while hearing another woman's voice. The infants showed comfort only when the situation righted itself.

The infant's reaction to certain familiar sounds after birth depends upon what stage during fetal life that sound was also heard. As we will see in Chapter 7, when fetuses under six months' gestation are repeatedly subjected to the loud noises of an airplane taking off, they adapt in such a way that after birth in the first days of life they will sleep right through it. But if the fetus hears the same loud noises continually at a point later than seven months in the womb, after birth the newborn will react with distress to those noises. However, as just discussed, a mother's frequent reading of a pleasant story late in pregnancy may result in her newborn's desire to hear the same story read over and over again.

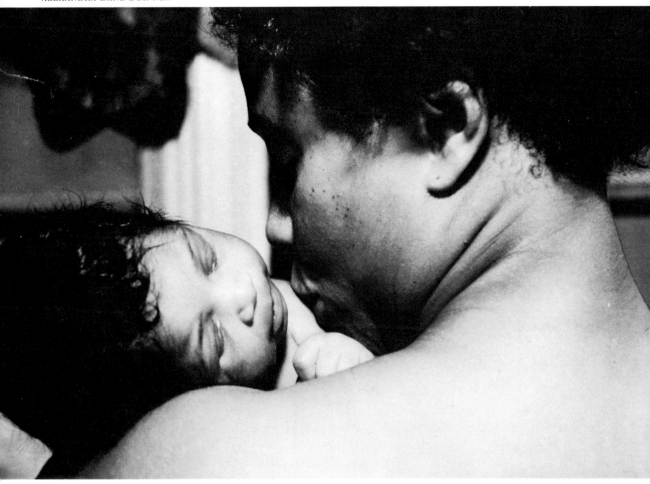

Shared touch is enjoyed by both mother and baby.

The skin is the largest sense organ of the body. *The sense of touch* is actuated early since babies are surrounded and caressed by warm fluid and tissues from the beginning of fetal life. They like closeness, warmth, and tactile comforting. They generally like to be cuddled and will often nestle and mold to your body. Parents all over the world naturally lift, hold, stroke, rock, and walk with their infant, as well as use other comforting touching motions to soothe the baby. Both parent and infant seem prepared to enjoy this experience.

55

**Newborn sleeping on his
father's chest**

Infants respond to other aspects of touch as well: variations in temperature, texture, moisture, pressure, pain. The lips and hands have the largest number of touch receptors; this may explain why newborns enjoy sucking their fingers. Ultrasound images show that unborn babies suck their thumbs as early as twenty-four weeks. The sense of touch is a major way that babies comfort themselves, explore their world, and initiate contact.

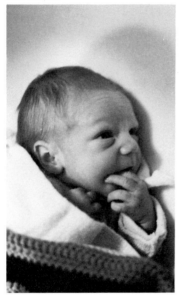

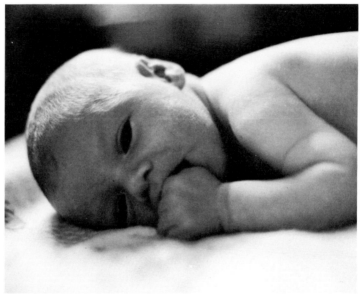

Newborns soothing themselves

As with other sense organs, *taste* is also highly developed in the infant at birth. Observations of what the newborn chooses to suck have shown that the infant is able to make fine discriminations and is responsive to small chemical alterations in the foods placed on their tongues. Infants show pleasure as sweetness is increased and displeasure with slightly salty, acidic, or bitter liquids.

ALEXANDRA DANE DOR-NER

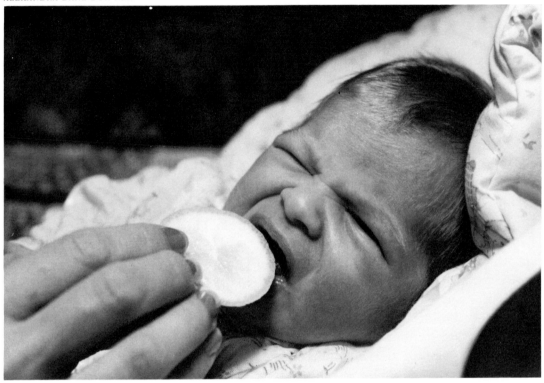

Infant tasting lemon

Babies can distinguish among and recognize different *smells*. After initially responding to new smells, they quickly adapt and stop responding once the smell becomes familiar. When a novel smell is presented, they show their interest by moving their heads; their activity level and heart rate change. By six days of life, babies will even recognize the smell of their own mother. Infant researcher Aidan Macfarlane in Oxford, England, explored this in detail. Using small gauze pads—the type that women who are breast-feeding use to absorb leaking milk—Macfarlane studied whether breast-feeding babies would recognize or turn toward their mother's pad versus choosing another mother's pad. He placed these pads on each side of the infant's face; one was the pad the mother wore, and the other was from another mother. He then watched the babies' reactions at two days of age; the breast-feeding babies did not show a preference for either pad. However, by six days of age, babies turned far more often to their mother's breast pad than to a clean breast pad or the breast pad of another mother. To be sure that the turning was not accidental, the location of the pads was changed every minute. The babies continued to turn toward their mother's pad—the pad marked X. The preference for the mother's breast pad became even more pronounced as the baby became older. Interestingly, though, when the mother's breast milk was placed on an unworn pad rather than an actual pad worn by the mother, the infants showed no preference. Apparently the babies respond to the special smell of the mother herself, not necessarily to the smell of the milk.

To test the ability of an infant to identify his own mother's odor, two breast pads—one belonging to his mother (marked X) and the other belonging to a stranger (plain)—are placed on either side of the baby's face.

The baby turns far to his left to his own mother's breast pad.

Furthermore, babies are not alone in being able to distinguish individuals by smell. If mothers are blindfolded and different babies are placed near their noses, they can identify their own baby. The sense of smell is one more way mother and baby learn about each other.

One of the most remarkable feats of the infant is the capacity to match information coming in from two different senses. This ability to process and store abstract information about objects has been studied mainly in three-week-old infants. Either a smooth or pebbly pacifier was slipped into the babies' mouths without their seeing what it looked like. The babies were given a minute and a half to become familiar with the pacifier. The pacifiers were then slipped out of their mouth, again without their seeing it. Next the babies were quickly shown two pictures of pacifiers, one pebbly and one smooth, as shown here. The observer used a device similar to the one employed by Dr. Fantz (Chapter 2) in order to see which picture the babies preferred. Surprisingly, the majority of babies

The pebbly and smooth pacifiers used to study the newborn's ability to recognize what is in his mouth

Nature, A. N. MELTZOFF AND R. W. BORTON

looked at the picture of the pacifier that they had had in their mouth. This suggests that somewhere in the infants' brain they are able to match the sensations they receive from mouthing an object with other sensations they receive when looking at the object — an incredible achievement for the brain of a human infant.

These unusual talents of the newborn may appear at different stages, disappear for a while, and reappear later. Some of this developmental process depends on need, use, underuse, overuse, passivity, and activity. When infants are pushed too much on the one hand, or deprived of various sensory stimuli on the other, their development may be affected. No one knows which skills need to be enhanced or which ones should be left alone. It is known, however, that infants take delight and interest in a variety of experiences; there is no right or perfect way to interact with them. By being attuned to their own infants, mothers and fathers soon learn what interests and amuses them and are able to discover enjoyable ways to interact.

4
·
Movement and Its Meaning

The myriad moving parts of a present-day automobile would have been incomprehensible to a man living ten thousand years ago. This strange machine would begin to make sense only if he could disassemble it and study the individual motions of the parts and their complexities, timing, and purpose. Modern-day scientists have been busy working on a similar venture to unravel the complexities of the seemingly purposeless movement of a newborn infant. Their recent findings form a fascinating picture. No longer are all the gestures and wriggles of a baby believed to be random or without meaning.

At times, while watching your newborn, try to see if there is any rhyme or reason to all the movements and gestures the baby makes. If your eye were a camera and able to perform time-lapse photography, one picture every second, you might make a rather astonishing discovery. Your baby moves in a very definite pattern when awake and not crying! For about one and a quarter minutes, there is no movement at all; then there is a burst of movement followed by a quiet period. This cycle of activity and quiet occurs continuously every one to two minutes when a newborn is in the active awake state of consciousness.

These motions are not the reflexive startles or jerks that sometimes occur in response to an environmental stimulus. Rather, there is an intrinsic rhythm to these spontaneous arm and leg movements that suggests there may be a clock in each infant's brain that directs this system. Attempting to discover how early and to what degree this rhythm is part of an organizational pattern in the nervous system of the infant, psychologist Dr. Steven Robertson found that the same type of spontaneous fluctuations in movement begin in the fetus as early as twenty weeks of pregnancy.

The amount of movement varies slightly for each baby, some infants moving much more or less than others; therefore, the range of total movement among normal newborns is large. Do not feel disappointed if you cannot see your own baby move in this rhythm because no one can time and observe this activity without special films. This pattern of motion, however, probably accounts for a large amount of your infant's arm and leg activity in the early months of life.

Perhaps these movements, which appear to be a reaching out and a drawing in of the arms and legs, are nature's way of helping you both learn about each other, an invitation by the baby for the adult to play and respond. Are remnants of these movements also possibly what makes it so hard for some young children at six years of age to sit still in school?

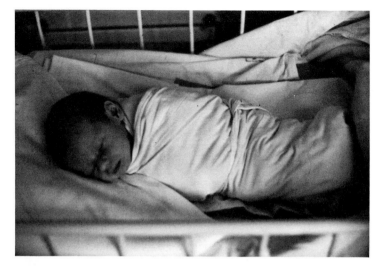

A Russian infant is being prepared in the hospital for swaddling. With swaddling, the infant's arms are placed snugly at her sides, and she is tightly wrapped in a traditional fashion.

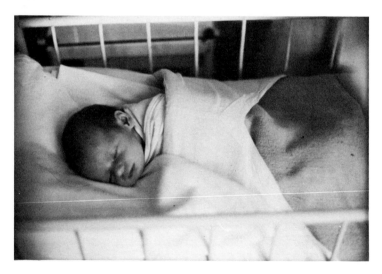

Additional blankets cover the infant when she sleeps.

Not only do babies show individuality in their activity levels, responses, and personalities, but different cultural practices and racial groups also affect how much a baby moves. For example, when babies are swaddled, they become quiet and move little. In these photos showing the swaddling of a Russian baby in a Moscow nursery, notice how tightly the arms are wrapped to the infant's sides and compare this with the freedom of Western babies. Not only do different cultural practices influence babies, but physical differences also appear to be present at birth. Observations of black, Caucasian, and Oriental newborns show that Oriental infants tend to have less muscle strength and tone and are also less active at birth than the other groups. By comparison, black infants in general have more muscle tone, strength, and activity than Oriental infants. Muscle tone of Caucasian infants falls somewhere in between that of black and Oriental infants. It is important to note, however, that as infants in all three groups grow, they develop a similar range of abilities.

Michael enjoying the free use of his arms

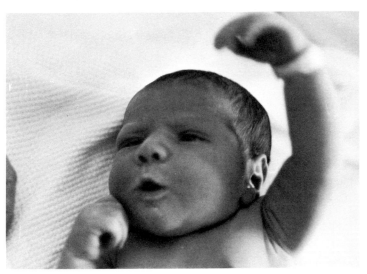

DAVID KLAUS

One of the most exciting observations about newborns' behavior is the movement of their bodies in synchrony to adult speech. Almost imperceptibly, a newborn baby's body moves in rhythm to its mother's voice, performing a kind of dance as the mother continues talking. The movements of this dance are not what you might expect. They might consist of the slight motion of an eyebrow lifting, a foot extending, or an arm raising. Notice here how each syllable elicits a new movement. The infant's moving body parts are coordinated with the elements of this woman's speech — even including the pauses or changes in the sound patterns.

A woman saying "pretty baby" to an infant illustrates that the infant's body moves in rhythm to speech.

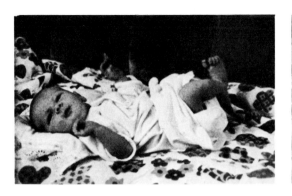

"PRET-"
The baby's arms and feet pull
back on the first syllable.

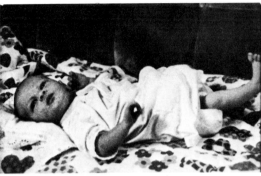

"-TY"
Her feet extend and her right
arm swings down on the second syllable.

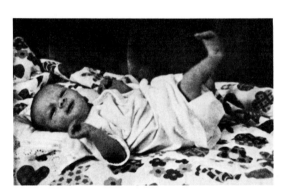

"BA-"
The baby's leg lifts up and
her arms pull back on the
third syllable.

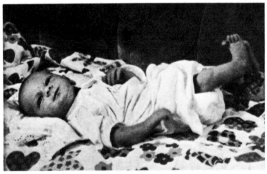

"-BY"
With the last syllable her
mouth closes, her feet extend
once more, a big toe wiggles,
and both arms lower.

This whole system, already present at birth, causes your infant to bend an ankle or lift an elbow or an eyebrow when you accent a syllable or pause for a breath. Such synchronous movements can be detected only with special film techniques. Newborns are somehow programmed to respond to human speech, and this is probably why young children are able to learn a foreign language much more readily than adults. How exactly this developed in your baby is a mystery, since American infants respond equally well to Chinese as they do to English. Tapping noises and disconnected vowel sounds, however, do not elicit corresponding infant movements.

All adults in all societies respond nonverbally as well as verbally to each other's speech. Listeners in any conversation move their body in rhythm with the speaker. These nonverbal movements are not recognized with the naked eye; however, we perceive them or "receive" them at an unconscious or subliminal level and they in turn may engage us to continue the communication. When you believe your baby is responding to you, you actually are "in tune" with each other. Your baby's *body* is prepared for a conversation with you long before he or she can say the words.

Many other responses that you observe daily in your newborn are, in large part, automatic and are termed "reflexes." You may have noticed that when you press your thumb into your infant's palm, the baby's mouth opens. This is called the Babkin reflex. Or, if you stroke the infant's cheek, the baby will turn in that direction and open her mouth. An infant comes into the world ready to eat, and this "rooting" reflex makes it easier to begin the feeding.

Preparing to press the infant's palms

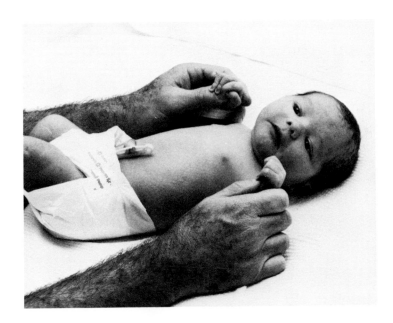

With light pressure on the infant's palms, her mouth opens.

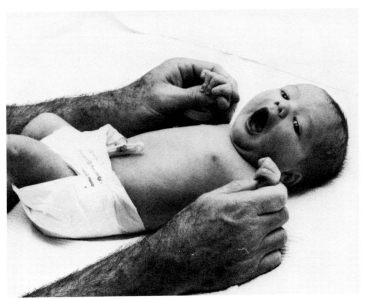

EDWARD CERUTTI, M.D.

69

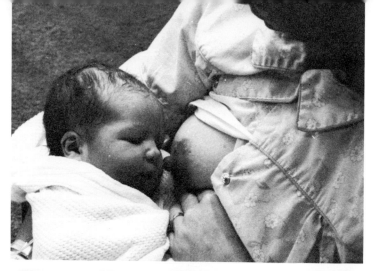

A mother initiates the rooting reflex in her infant girl
by lightly touching her nipple
to the baby's cheek.

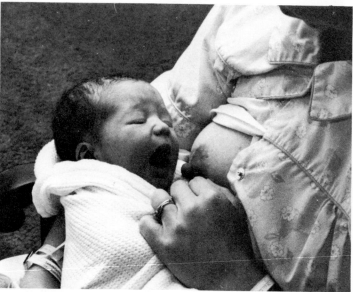

With the touch on her cheek,
the baby's mouth opens
widely.

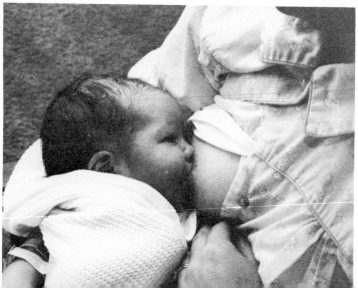

She immediately begins to
nurse.

Notice, too, how tightly your newborn can grasp your finger. Newborns can even hold their own weight under certain circumstances and with help will pull to a sitting position. Some scientists think that the grasp reflex represents an evolutionary adaptation because it would have allowed the infant to hold onto the mother's hair during prolonged hikes or while escaping from danger. A baby's toes attempt to grasp in a similar fashion.

Five-minute-old girl (the first of twins) grasps her father's finger

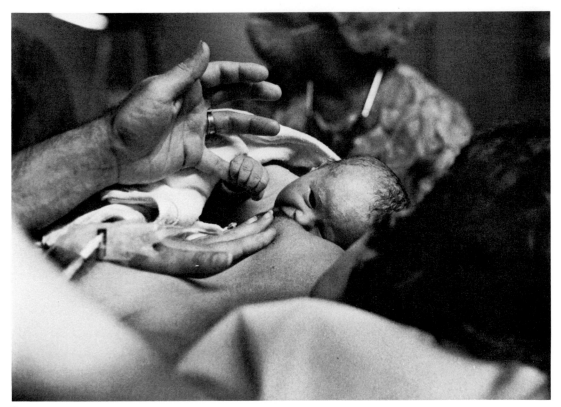

© SUZANNE ARMS

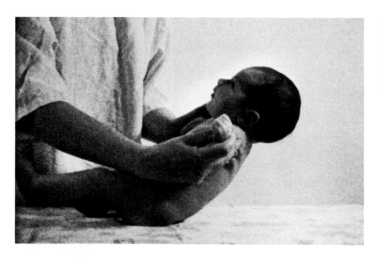

This premature baby grasps a nurse's fingers and is able to support his head and weight as he is gently pulled to a sitting position.

When sitting, he balances his head.

After being lowered, he startles and extends his arms and legs. The well-known Moro reflex is seen when the infant is put down suddenly or startled: the arms and legs move out abruptly and then inward slightly.

Another automatic motion occurs when infants are held upright with their feet touching the top of a table—they will make stepping movements, just as though they were about to walk.

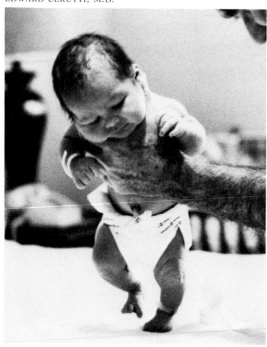 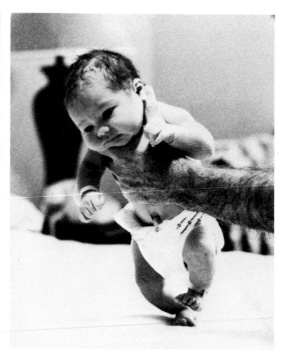

Alyson at nine hours old walks on the table with some support. First she steps with her left foot.

Then she steps with her right foot and lifts her left foot up to step again.

 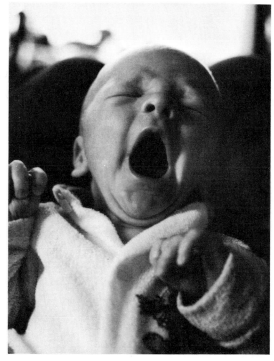

A great yawn

Infants share other automatic reflexes with adults. Their heart responds to emotional changes, such as fear, with an increased heartbeat. They sneeze when you tickle their nose with a feather, cough and gag when food goes down the wrong way, and often have a large bowel movement after a big meal. They also have formidable yawns.

The random reflex arm and leg movements that you notice in your baby in the active awake state have made many believe that newborns are too immature to have the capacity to reach for objects. Babies do not generally start to reach for objects until they are about four months old. Formerly, nerve physiologists explained this inability to reach by the absence of an insulating cover around each nerve. This theory was invalidated when two French pediatricians with a great deal of research experience, C. Amiel-Tison and A. Grenier, demonstrated that some newborns could reach. With the infant in the quiet alert state, looking face to face, attentive and still, they gently rubbed its neck for three to five minutes, permitting the neck muscles to relax and freeing the infant to reach. One out of every two newborns studied were actually able to reach for objects at a few days of age. Normal newborns at birth apparently have the underlying ability to reach. However, they have very strong neck muscles that are linked to their arms, causing any slight movement of the neck to also move their arms. This arm-and-neck reflex protects the baby's head from falling, but it also prevents the baby from reaching unless the neck muscles are very relaxed.

After hearing of the work of these pediatricians, we searched our films and realized that we had unknowingly filmed this reaching ability in one of the infants we had studied.

In the photographs shown here, see if you can notice this one-day-old baby reaching for her father's finger. When we first viewed this, our "prejudiced" eye saw only the father putting his finger into the baby's grasping hand. However, on viewing this at very slow speed, over and over again, we realized that it showed something quite different. The infant, in reality, is following and reaching out for the father's finger. The movement of the father's and infant's fingers can be followed by noting their position relative to the vertical lines of the bedspread. The baby in fact did this twice. It is interesting how our fixed beliefs can prevent us from noticing what actually may be happening.

After getting his one-day-old baby's attention, a father and daughter play a finger game. The father reaches toward, but does not touch, the baby's hand; then he pulls his finger back and the baby begins to reach for his finger.

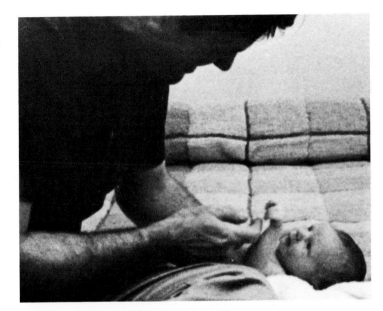

She continues to follow his finger past the line on the couch while he continues to pull his hand back.

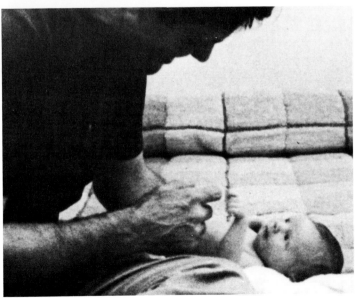

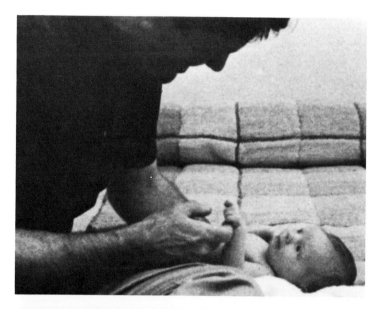

She finally grasps his finger.

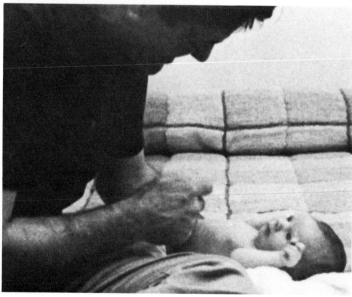

They both pull away.

She again reaches for his finger.

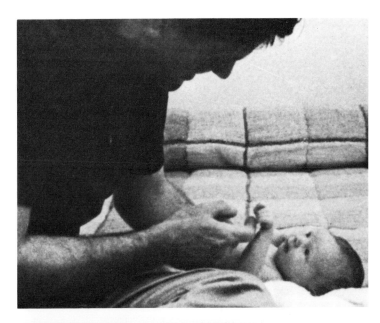

While he is pulling back, she grasps his finger again.

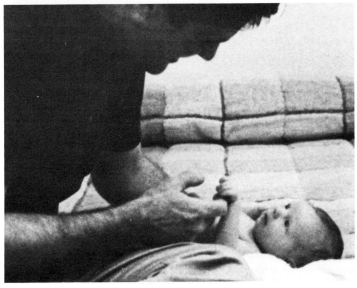

We would like to caution readers that this reaching will be seen only rarely in infants. Even the original French studies found this in only one-half of the perfectly normal bright babies tested, and we can find it in even fewer. We are describing this with a bit of trepidation because we fear that parents will be disappointed if they cannot see this in their own baby. This is a rare occurrence, not easily seen unless filmed with special techniques. Trying to encourage this reaching will not improve your baby's talents or abilities.

We believe that the parents' own feelings and sensitivities to the infant's needs and pace form the ideal environment for the infant's natural development to unfold. We mention reaching ability only to suggest that once in a while, when you play a finger game with your baby, the baby may actually be reaching for your finger rather than the reverse.

As you watch your baby's fascinating array of motions, patient attention will help you sort them out. One set of wiggles could be the result of that automatic timer setting the newborn off every minute and a half. Certain repeated motions could be the result of automatic reflexes. More rhythmic patterns might indicate that the baby is moving in tune to your words. On rare occasions, motion could reflect an attempt to reach out to you; or, quite simply, perhaps the baby is moving an arm or leg because the position is uncomfortable. When the baby is asleep, as mentioned earlier, movement could mean the baby is dreaming. Exploring these various motions and their meanings is another way of getting to know your newborn.

5
·

Facial
Expressions
·

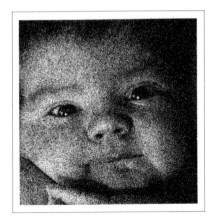

The faces of human infants have a special fascination for most adults. The broad forehead, large shiny eyes, tiny nose, and softness of the skin are like a magnetic force that attracts men and women as well as children. The universal appeal of these characteristics has even been exaggerated by Walt Disney in his famous cartoon figures, Donald Duck and Mickey Mouse. Not surprisingly, tape recordings of mothers' reactions when alone for the first time with their infant reveal that nearly 80 percent of what they say relates to the face of the baby—especially the eyes.

Just as you are interested in your baby's face, the baby, in turn, arrives in the world with a special fascination for your face. When newborns are shown comparisons of a human face and an abstract design, they prefer the human face. When quiet and alert, babies will often gaze at your face with special interest or pleasure and are capable not only of responding to what they see in your face but actually of imitating some of your expressions. A talented Greek psychologist, Olga Maratos, first noted this capacity to imitate.

Ben and his mother. Who is imitating whom?

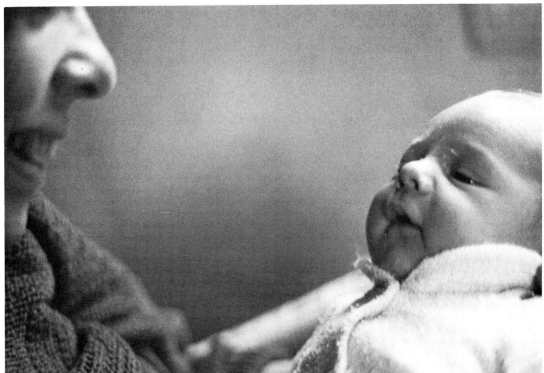

Try this yourself. With the baby in a quiet alert state, about eight to ten inches away from you, and looking directly at your face, slowly protrude your tongue as far as you can. Repeat the tongue protrusion slowly every twenty seconds, six to eight times; then stop. The baby, if she continues to look at your face, often may begin to move her own tongue in her mouth. The baby may first move it against one inside cheek; then after twenty or thirty seconds, her tongue will slowly appear at her lips and, finally, sometimes be pushed far out of the mouth. This will work only if you protrude your tongue while the baby's attention is on your face. A word of caution: babies have minds of their own and may not choose to play this game.

When Leah is looking directly at her face, her mother protrudes her tongue.

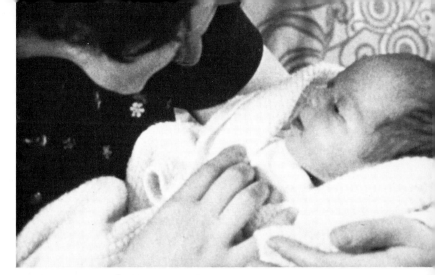

After about thirty to forty-five seconds, Leah tenses her body slightly and begins to push her tongue out.

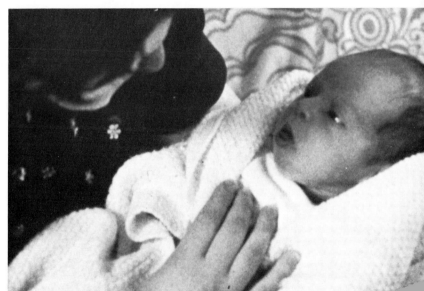

Leah is now imitating her mother.

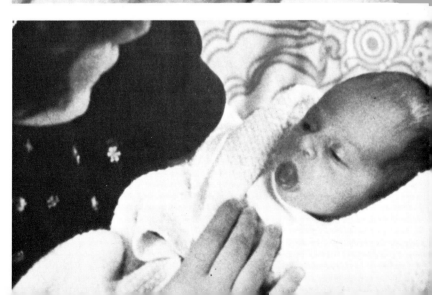

The baby below is imitating Professor Andrew Meltzoff, who has studied this ability in great detail. Here the baby is imitating the tongue protruding, opening the mouth, and pursing the lips. These three imitations were done at separate sessions.

Science, A. N. MELTZOFF AND M. K. MOORE

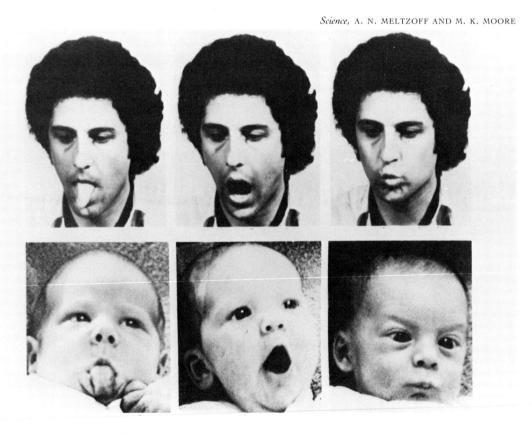

A young infant imitating Professor Meltzoff protrudes his tongue, opens his mouth, and purses his lips. Each gesture was done at a different time.

During a teaching visit to China, we recently observed an unusual example of this ability. While we were demonstrating a newborn's various talents, I asked a revered older professor to play the tongue protrusion game with an eight-hour-old Chinese baby girl. As the professor slowly stuck out her tongue, then waited the appropriate time, the baby began to protrude her tongue. All twelve Chinese doctors and nurses were delighted. Then I showed the baby around the circle one by one so the staff and infant could view one another, and I asked the doctors and nurses not to stick out their tongues. When the baby again came face-to-face with the revered professor, the baby immediately protruded her tongue, even though the professor made no facial expression or movements. Everyone gasped! So we decided to try it again. Each time we went away from the baby, went to examine other infants, and then came back to the first baby, she stuck out her tongue only for the older professor and without any prompting! The memory trace of the older professor appeared indelibly etched in the mind of that little newborn girl.

How do babies accomplish such a remarkable feat? They must somehow sense that they have a tongue as you do, as well as where it is located and how to control it. The act of imitation is a complex affair. It is wonderful to realize that a newborn infant—never having looked in a mirror, never having played the toddler game of finding her own nose or her mother's nose—somehow recognizes that what she is seeing in your face relates to a part of her own body!

This game can affect the behavior of both mother and baby in strange ways. A mother described to me how first her baby yawned, inspiring her to yawn, then the baby yawned again, and so on until they both fell asleep.

The facial expressions of newborns are strikingly similar across all cultures. It seems that when expressing the common emotions of fear, sadness, joy, disgust, and anger, the human face speaks a universal language. From the newborn period on, photographs taken of babies show that infants are capable of producing almost all of the adult facial expressions of specific emotions. The photograph at right shows a sad expression on a baby less than one hour old.

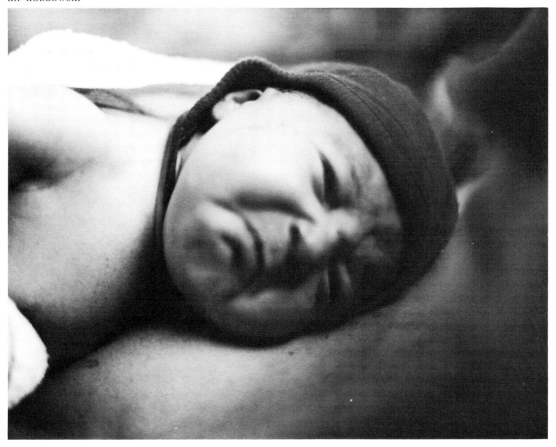

**Zach, one hour old, shows a
sad expression.**

The baby's face shown here reflects the emotions of sadness, surprise, and happiness as he imitates a model's face. This study of babies' imitation of emotions was undertaken by Professor Tiffany Field and her colleagues. An adult modeled a series of three facial expressions (sadness, happiness, and surprise) to a group of newborn infants. An observer standing behind the adult model was not able to view the model's face and therefore did not know which expressions were being demonstrated. As he watched, the observer noted on paper what facial expressions he thought the baby was imitating. (Both the infant's and the adult model's faces were videotaped to provide a later check on the observer's notations.)

Below: An infant imitating a sad expression. Top right: The same infant imitating an expression of surprise. Bottom right: The same baby imitating a happy expression.

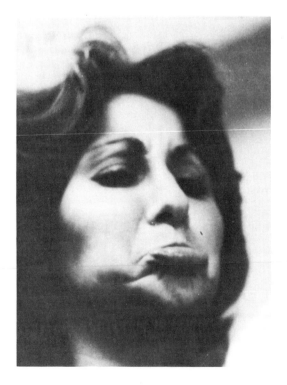 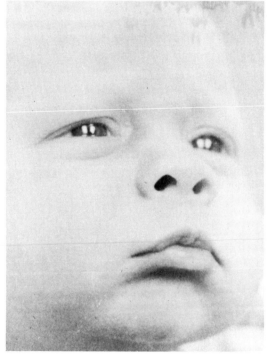

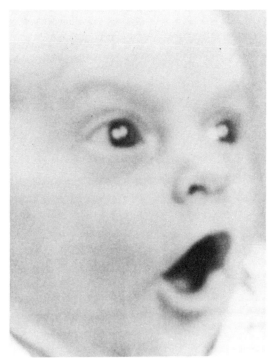

Newborns will focus their eyes on the eyes and mouth of the adult as they watch their expressions. Infants will then change their own eyes and mouths according to what they see. Notice the widening of the eyes and the mouth when they imitate the expression of surprise, while they pull in the brows and protrude the mouth in imitation of the sad expression. It is not known when newborns experience inner feelings related to the emotions they are imitating. Perhaps an innate ability in human infants to link what they see with what they sense in their own faces, along with the natural mobility and activity of their features, account for the newborn's capacity to produce a broad range of facial expressions. As babies become older, their faces show expressions commonly shared by their particular family and culture to express genuine emotions. It is not uncommon to recognize an expression on your infant's face that reminds you of someone in the family.

A variety of expressions in a baby boy

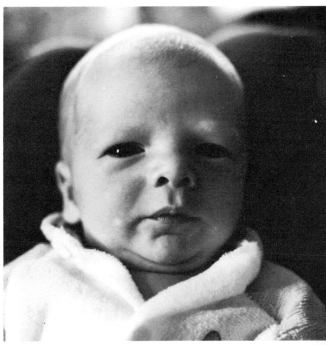
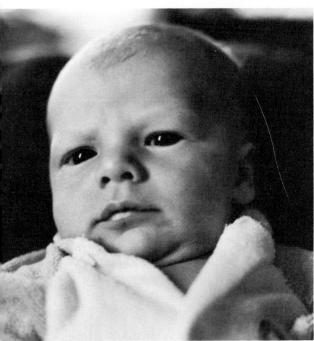
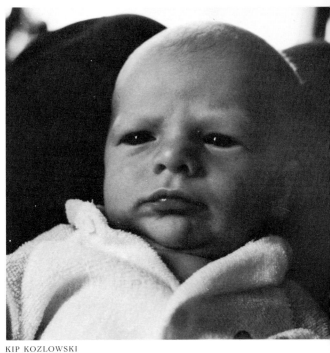

KIP KOZLOWSKI

"SCHOOL OF MIDWIFERY",
East Glamorgan General Hospital,
Church Village,

It is worth noting that during the entire time the baby is beginning to find herself in her mother's face, the mother herself is making many adjustments to the infant's face. Mothers-to-be often dream of their baby and near the end of pregnancy will begin to develop a particular mental image of the infant. At the earliest moment of acquaintance after birth, mothers begin to replace the imagined baby with their real baby. Not only is there likely to be a marked difference between the expected and the real facial features, but the activity and behavior of the baby may also differ from a mother's expectations.

Intricacies of the relationship between the mother and infant have been much illuminated by the perceptive observations of Dr. D. W. Winnicott, a well-known English psychiatrist. He observed that mothers are a mirror for their babies and spend much time in the first months of life imitating their infants. Dr. Winnicott commented on the mirror role of the mother: "What does the baby see when he or she looks at the mother's face? I am suggesting that, ordinarily, what the baby sees is himself or herself. In other words, the mother is looking at the baby and what she looks like is related to what she sees there. All this is too easily taken for granted. I am asking that this which is naturally done well by mothers who are caring for their babies shall not be taken for granted!" Thus both the mother and infant imitate each other. This process of pacing yourself to your infant becomes especially important as the infant is beginning to discover her own being or boundaries.

Babies appear to become more responsive as mothers gently follow or imitate them rather than stimulate or lead them. Once an individual has a well-integrated sense of self or personhood, that person is likely to become upset if imitated. However, an infant's self is incompletely formed; the boundaries between the infant and others are not clear to the baby. Imitation of the infant's actions aids the process of self-discovery. After periods of active responding, babies tend to quiet down or turn off for a while—perhaps to rest, since too much play, either imitation or stimulation, tires them. This mutual mirroring is yet another way that infants learn about themselves, learn about you, and learn about how to act in their society. It is not a deliberate, self-conscious activity but takes place at an almost unaware level of consciousness. We describe the process only because it is fun to know what is going on, not because either you or your baby have to be coached; it comes naturally.

As parents spend time getting to know their baby, they gradually learn to put themselves in their infant's place. When they do, the signals the baby sends out to make his or her needs known or to elicit a response become increasingly clear. Within us all are amazing inborn systems for communicating, nurturing, and surviving.

6
·
The Newborn in the Family
·

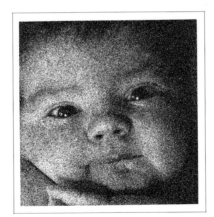

The incredible attributes of the newborn have a major purpose. They prepare the baby for interaction with the family and for life in the world. This newborn girl is ready to gaze upon, cuddle close to, listen to, and feed from her mother.

An infant at twenty minutes of age looks intensely at her mother.

© SUZANNE ARMS

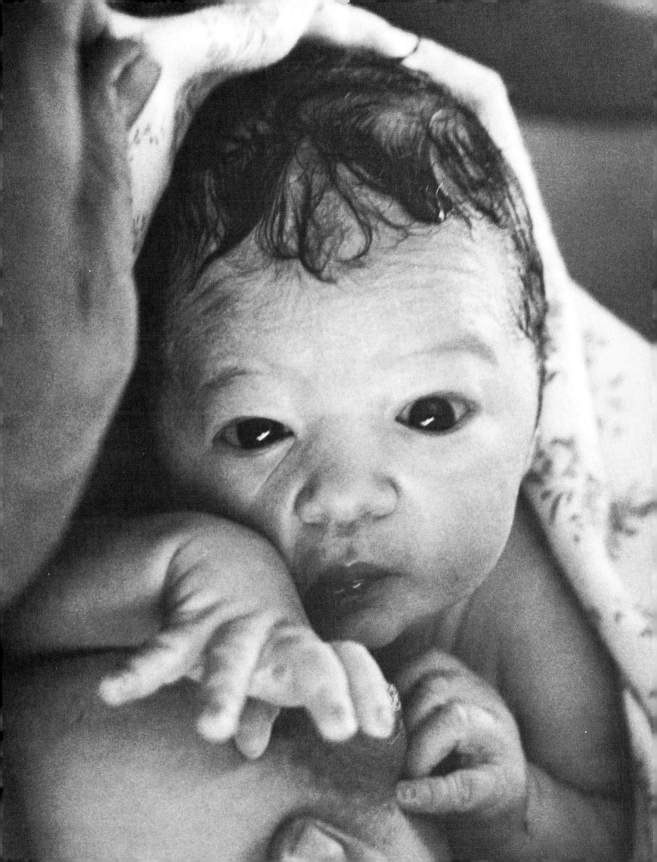

Nature also activates each member of the family in unique ways to receive the baby. When holding their infants for the first time, mothers almost invariably explore their babies in a particular order. They begin initially to touch the infant's arms and legs with their fingertips in a fashion somewhat similar to a cook testing a cake to see if it is finished. After a few minutes, and sometimes even a few seconds, many mothers proceed to massage, touch, and stroke their infant's body. Fathers start the process of getting to know their babies in similar ways.

A father and mother begin to explore their infant.

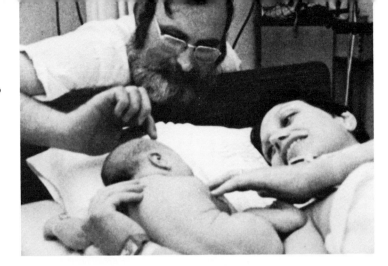

They continue to lightly touch their baby.

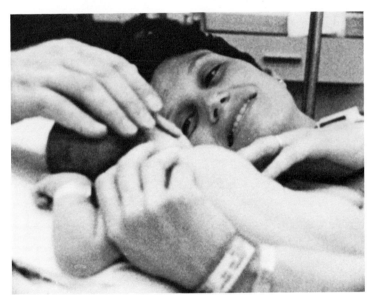

They then begin to stroke the baby's trunk.

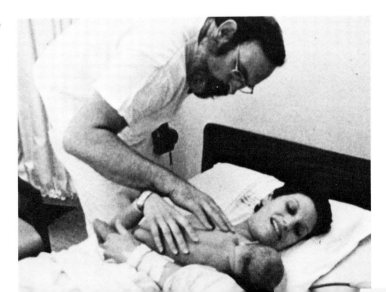

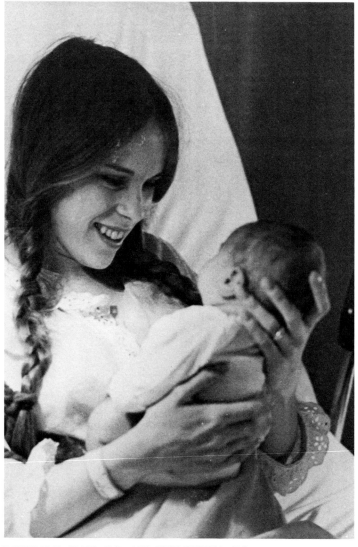

A mother aligns her face and the baby's on the same parallel plane (*en face*).

MARSHALL H. KLAUS, M.D., AND JOHN KENNELL, M.D.

At this very early time, parents have a special interest in the infant's eyes and unconsciously try to align their faces on the same parallel plane of rotation as their infant's. This is called the *en face* position, or face-to-face. We have observed this not only with parents getting to know their full-term babies, but also with mothers and fathers of premature babies. In the nursery for prematures, mothers have to tilt their heads a great deal to move themselves into the *en face* position.

A mother of a premature infant tilts her head to align it with her infant's.

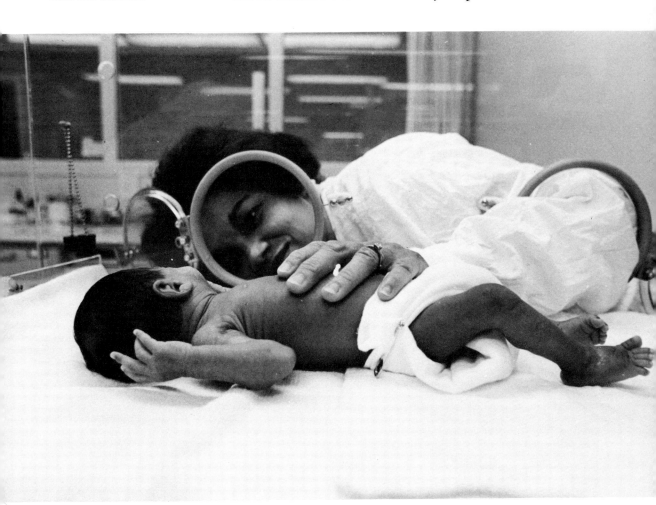

103

These tentative early greetings are accompanied by a tide of new feelings. During the first hour of life, as already noted, there is an extended period of quiet alertness in the newborn infant. The infant looks at the mother's face, follows, and responds to her voice. Mothers and fathers often express an unusual sense of excitement when they begin to make contact with their babies. Many mothers report feeling warmly close to their infants after the infant has looked at them, acknowledging the importance of relating to the baby through eye contact. More than one mother has said, "Open your eyes, oh come on, open your eyes. If you open your eyes, I'll know you're mine."

A mother's very early view of her newborn

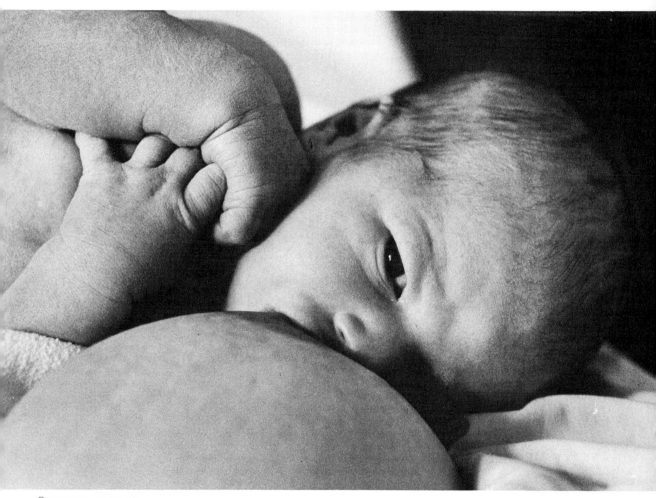

© THOMAS BERGMAN

Many mothers find these early periods together especially rewarding for another reason. Some women fear that they might give birth to an infant that is not perfect. They cannot believe that they are good enough to produce a completely normal infant. For these mothers, as well as fathers with similar fears, these early private times together replace some of the anxieties parents feel at birth with a sense of grateful wonder.

Some parents who miss these early periods with their infants or do not feel an immediate love for their baby believe that they cannot be bonded or attached to their baby in a normal fashion or that something is lost in their future relationship with the baby. Such doubts are unfounded. In spite of the fact that, for the past thirty or forty years, most parents who gave birth in hospitals lacked early contact with their babies, almost all of these parents nevertheless became bonded and attached to their children. Many people misunderstand the process of bonding and give too literal a meaning to the word "bonding." Some skeptic called this literal interpretation the "epoxy model." The process of becoming attached to one's infant occurs at different times for different people. For some parents, it develops during pregnancy; for other parents, it happens during the first moments after birth; and for many others, not until they are home from the hospital taking care of their infants for the first time alone.

Fully 40 percent of perfectly normal mothers take a week or longer to feel the baby is truly theirs. The same is true for fathers of newborns. Some germane comments that we have recorded over the years follow:

"My husband, particularly after we had the first visit with the baby, said, 'He's ours, I know he's ours, and I love him very much.' I knew I loved him, but it took me a little bit longer to realize that this baby was ours."

"Until he was in our home and I was taking care of him I didn't feel he was mine."

Another mother, moments after birth, said, "That he was real is overwhelming. Somehow when he's inside he's real but isn't real and then when he's on the outside you have to think, my goodness, it really is a baby and somehow it's a surprise. He was looking us over and looking the world over. It was a two-way kind of thing that fascinated me. He was responding to us but he was a stranger. I was delighted to have him but in some ways we were discovering each other with the child. We were a threesome."

"There was a rush of feelings after delivery, you could hear him and he was real. I could still see the connection between him and me. He was so beautiful and he was OK." This woman's husband said, "I was surprised at how he looked, I really hadn't any mental image of what he would look like. It was just like a lump in her belly and here it was a person."

Dr. Winnicott's description of "primary maternal preoccupation" is helpful in understanding this period of life for the mother. "It is a state of heightened sensitivity that lasts for a few weeks after the birth . . . [which] provides a setting for the infant's individuality to make itself evident, for the developmental tendencies to start to unfold, and for the infant to become the owner of the sensations that are appropriate to this early phase of life. A mother who is in this state can feel herself into her infant's place."

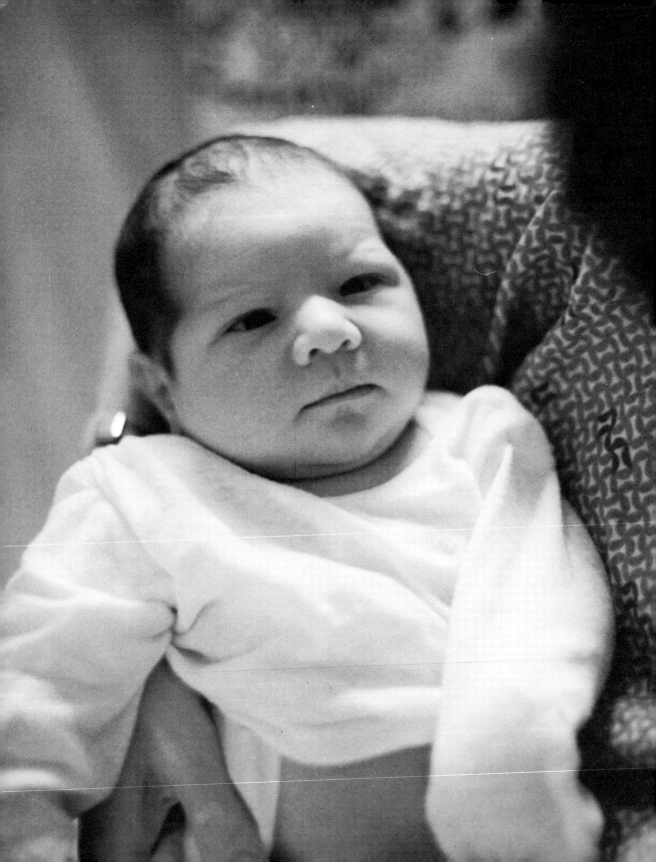

Michael looking at his mother

An amazing mutuality pervades the relationship between the mother and the newborn. The mother appears to be especially open and unusually receptive in the first weeks of her child's life to learning about and perceiving her infant through all her senses. The infant's talents, abilities, and wide range of senses described in the previous chapters are each matched by parallel sensitivities and alertness on the part of the mother. There is a mutual interest in eye-to-eye contact. A mother's use of a high-pitched voice in talking to her infant coincides with the infant's attraction to speech in the high-frequency range. The timing of speech stimulates both the parent and infant to move to its rhythm. An infant's cry will stimulate milk production. As we saw before, during bottle- or breast-feeding, the distance between the parent and the infant's eyes is about eight to ten inches, an optimum distance for a newborn to see his mother, or in some cases, his father. Not only does the breast milk transmit defenses against infection to the baby, but the infant's sucking action causes hormones to be produced in the mother that help return her uterus to its former shape. A feedback loop pervades the relationship between mother and baby on several levels.

The baby lets you know he is with you in other subtle ways as well. For example, when a baby is feeding and parents start to talk, the baby stops sucking or changes his sucking rate as he tries to listen. These pauses occur mainly at hearing the mother's voice, not other sounds. The baby rewards the mother for fondling, kissing, cuddling, and prolonged gazing by looking into her eyes, smiling, turning to her voice, and quieting to her touch. Mother and infant, especially suited to each other physiologically, hormonally, and emotionally, respond to each other on a number of sensory and social levels that serve to lock the pair together. Many parents look back upon this early time of closeness as deeply joyful and meaningful.

Two newborns resting against their mothers' knees, looking at them, and listening intently

SCOTT SHAGIN

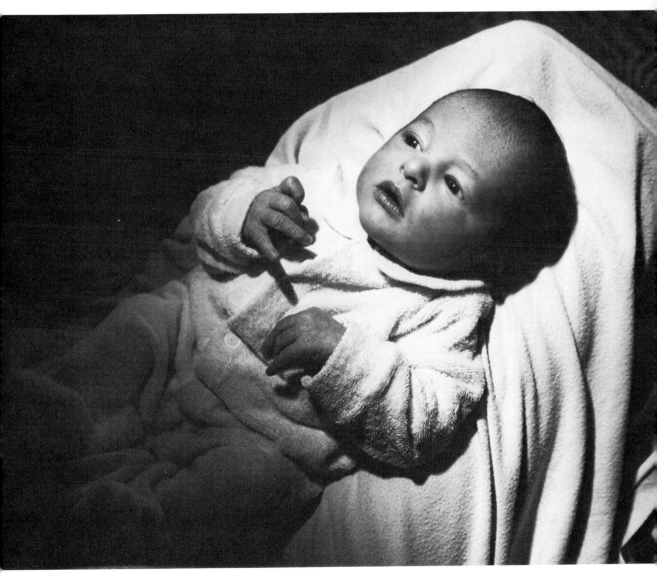

The more time parents can spend with their infant in the first few days in the hospital, the better they will understand the baby and be able to meet the newborn's needs once they are at home. Fathers can also derive great pleasure from these early hours and days with their babies. As time goes on, they have a different style from mothers. Video-tapes have shown how fathers tend to be more active and playful with their infants than mothers, and how babies learn early to anticipate the fun. Grandparents need little encouragement to enjoy a new baby and early contact helps them feel close as well.

This infant seems to be registering surprise upon meeting his grandmother.

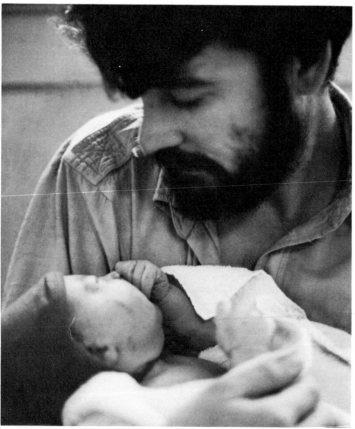

Zach and his father in the first hour of life

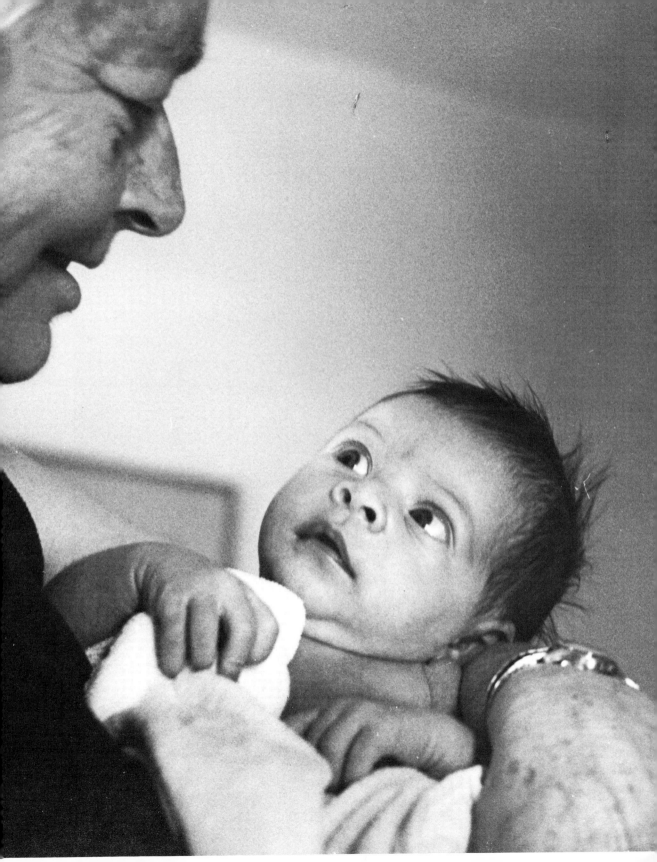

N. JAY JAFFEE

A baby girl meets her grandfather.

Once the infant is home, the father has a much easier time taking care of the infant and getting to know him. One father's own words describe what can happen. "He's so communicative. His typical pattern is to wake up and nurse a bit and then I'll take him in and change him and he's good on the changing table. By then, he's bright eyed and alert and he just really takes in everything around him and he'll focus on you and you get really great eye contact with him. He responds to your talking and if he fusses a little bit, I pick him up, he always calms down and there's an eye communication, and there's body-to-body communication, a patting, a comforting, and he's a very responsive kid. I don't think I ever expected that at so young an age."

It is interesting that the way the father shown here instinctively soothes his baby is the method that changes most infants from crying to the quiet alert state.

A father comforts his sixteen-minute-old girl.

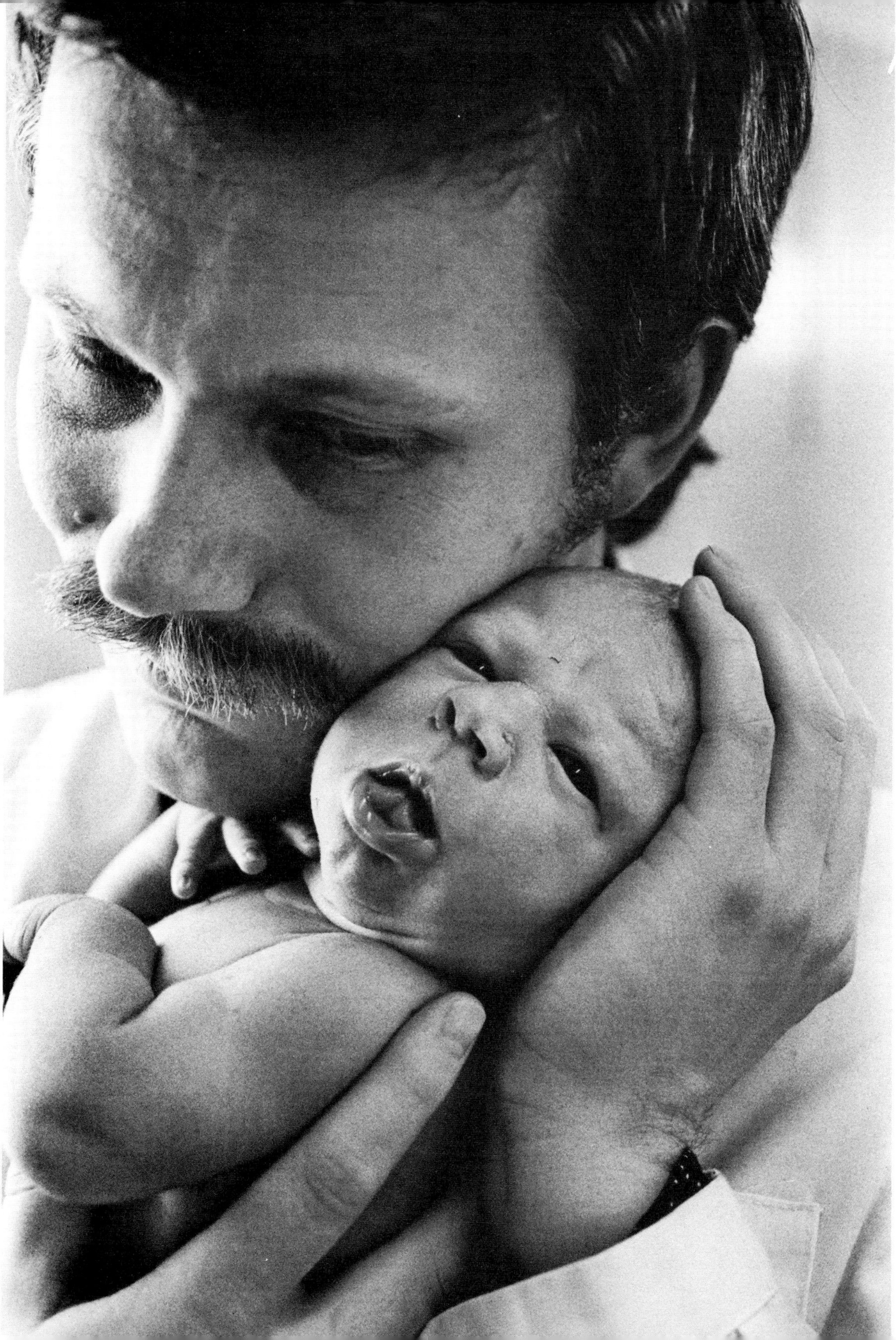

118

A two-year-old boy inspects his three-hour-old sister.

For years mothers have complained about being torn between the new baby in the hospital and the young child who is already at home. For a child under six, the short separation from the mother can seem like a very long time. Since young children have a different concept of time than adults, they sometimes believe they have been abandoned for an extended period, when they have actually been separated from their mother for only a few days. This short separation commonly results in temper tantrums, sleep disturbances, and eating problems for the child.

Siblings, too can benefit from the earliest possible contact with the newborn. It is recommended that siblings visit their mother daily. The photograph below shows the beginning of a visit.

Katie visits her mother for the first time after the birth of her sister.

Parents sometimes doubt whether a sibling should come to the hospital because little children often cry when the visit is over. However, the benefits far outweigh the relatively short-lived distress that occurs when the young child must leave. It is important to remember that the young siblings are coming in to see their mother first and foremost and only secondarily to see the infant. Mothers should take a little time to play alone with the older child before they visit the baby. The photographs at right show the next portion of the same visit.

Katie's first view of her sister through the glass wall of the nursery. With a rather wistful expression, she tries to align her head with her new sister's.

Katie says goodbye.

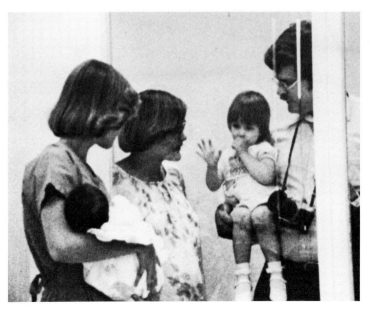

Most maternity hospitals are making major changes in visiting practices, such as allowing the older child more frequent visits with the mother and arranging for the child to stay for a meal. When the older sibling has been more involved with the newborn during the hospital stay, the homecoming is often less fraught with anxieties. These photographs show the same older sister exploring the new baby on the first day home. As babies get older, they begin to show a special fascination for other children, for someone clearly closer to their own size. The awestruck gaze of a baby can help win over the most skeptical older brother or sister.

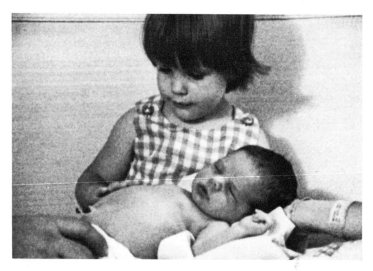

With guidance, Katie holds her sister at home for the first time. She touches the baby's abdomen.

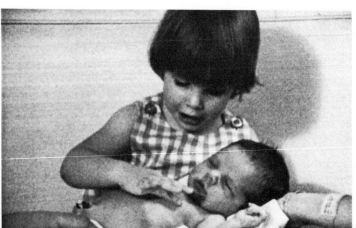

She touches one nipple.

Katie now examines her sister's right nipple.

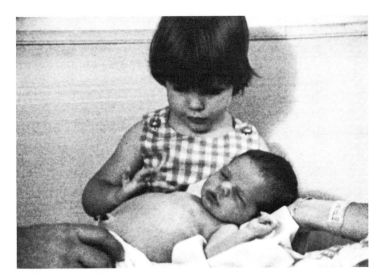

She compares the baby with herself.

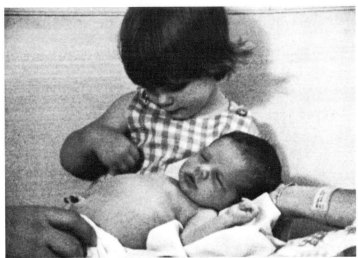

Katie moves closer and hugs her sister.

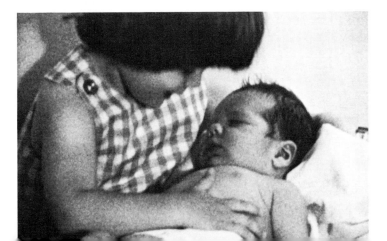

A father holds his baby tenderly.

This is only the beginning in the complex process by which families become attached to their newborn infant. Mothers and fathers can expect an ever-increasing range of responses as the infant grows. A Mayan Indian saying tells us: "In the baby lies the future of the world. The mother must hold him close so he will know the world is his. The father must take him to the highest hill so he can see what his world is like."

7

·

Before Birth: The Dawn of Awareness

·

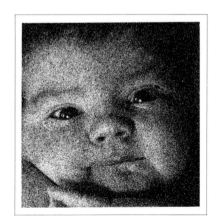

As discussed, in the first minutes following birth, human babies already have an extraordinary ability to interact with their parents. To understand how and when this full array of senses came to be developed, it is necessary to look back to very early fetal life. The world of the human fetus is alive with activity, with special rhythms, with movements that have purpose, with senses that are beginning to work — seeing, hearing, tasting, and being touched — and with complex responses to the emotions and actions of its mother.

A newborn ready for his parents

© MIMI COTTER

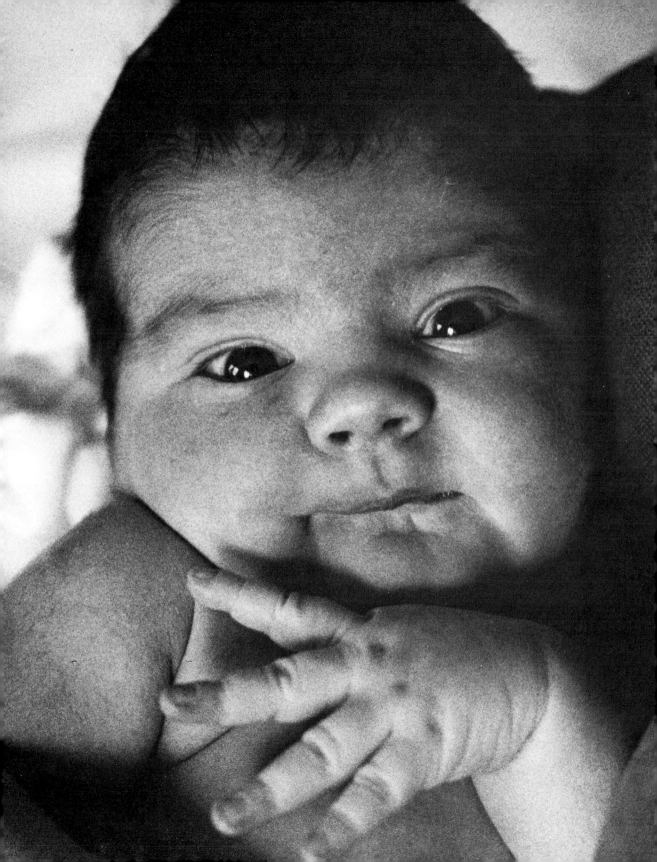

Years ago the growing fetus was thought to live in an isolated world, an impenetrable castle, impervious to the environment outside its mother's womb. Our notion of what life is like for the human fetus has changed. Ultrasound images and other innovative technologies, as well as careful observations of very premature infants who survived early delivery, have given us a glimpse into the life of the fetus and its capacities to react, to perceive light and sound, to register sensations or sensory messages. We know much more about how intrauterine experience and activities rehearse and prepare the fetus for life outside the uterus.

Ultrasound was first developed during World War II and used extensively to detect enemy submarines. Sound waves are transmitted through water, and as they bounce off an object are reflected back and projected by a computerized technique onto a screen. The ultrasound devices presently used to study the fetus can reveal exquisite details of its body. A small, lightweight instrument placed on the mother's abdomen sends and receives the sound waves. After these waves bounce off the fetus, they are projected onto a screen that can show both still and moving pictures. As an example, the photograph shown here is the face of a twenty-week-old fetus.

Though ultrasound is probably safe, not everything about its effect is yet known. Most doctors recommend that it be used only when necessary. In practice ultrasound is used mainly to estimate the age of the fetus by measuring the dimensions of its head. This is most accurate when done between fifteen and thirty weeks of pregnancy. It is also used to check for certain problems in development.

JASON BIRNHOLZ/ELAINE FARREL

An ultrasound profile of the face of a twenty-week-old fetus

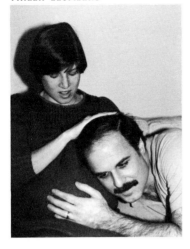

A father tries to hear the fetus.

Through this window into the womb we can follow the growth of the fetus from its beginning weeks of life. By means of an ultrasound image, one can see that a five-week-old fetus is capable of spontaneous movement.

Mothers first begin to feel the fetus move at about four to five months of pregnancy, and fathers—when they rest their hands on the mother's abdomen—shortly after that. However, undetected motion already has been occurring for some time. By seven to eight weeks, the fetus can accomplish very simple movements of a single arm or leg joint, the wrist, elbow, or knee. At twelve weeks, the fetus can move all the joints of an arm or leg together. By thirteen to fourteen weeks, the arms may move with the legs, and sometimes the fetus can even be seen to hold its hands up. By nineteen weeks, the fetus can step, hold itself erect, and scoot itself forward by bracing against a hand. Such abilities have been seen both in ultrasound images and in tiny premature babies.

This father, like many others, wonders if he can detect any movement of the fetus through his wife's abdomen.

Looking from the back of this thirteen-week-old fetus's head, you can see both arms upraised.

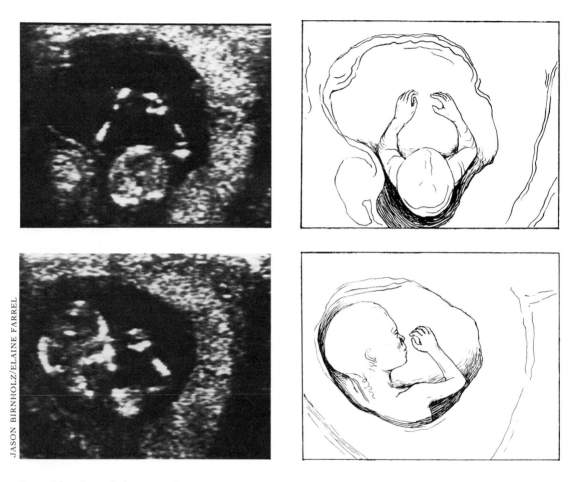

In a side view of the same fetus, you can see it raise a hand toward its face.

This astonishing repertoire of motions has many purposes. Motion itself is essential for the growth and development of the muscles and bones as well as for the stimulation of nerve-cell growth in the brain. An extension of the nerve cells in the brain actually grows into an arm or a leg. Motion helps this growth and, at the same time, creates new pathways for future nerves. This process, for example, permits children as they grow to develop very fine hand control. The movements of arms and legs can be compared to the work of a shuttle in a loom that weaves through the warp of the fabric, adding a new row of thread to the cloth with each motion. If movement is prevented in any limb, the joint freezes, muscles and nerves wither, and the bone atrophies. Thus the movements you feel as a pregnant parent are crucial for your baby's development.

These four images show a moving arm and hand of a thirty-three-week-old fetus. Is it sucking its thumb?

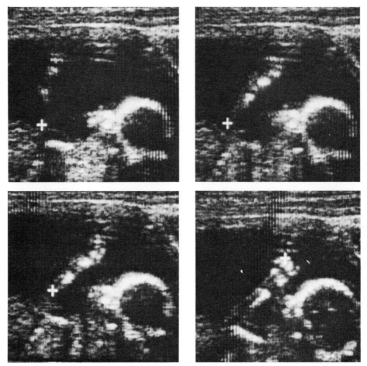

The fetus lives in the amniotic sac, a fluid-filled container that cushions and protects it. In this floating and weightless environment, the limbs and body have a wide range of freedom to move, keeping the joints flexible. The rocking motions that the baby experiences in utero may explain why, after birth, the newborn derives so much pleasure from being held and rocked.

As researchers have observed the fetus using ultrasound, they have noticed a variety of unexpected behavior. Yawning, swallowing, breathing, rooting, smiling, grimacing, sucking, grasping, stretching, curling, and unfolding appear to be practiced for long periods before they are necessary. This rehearsal, like the training of an athlete, helps make each motion more smooth and coordinated over time.

The fetus develops its own rhythms and patterns. The activities and life of the fetus are governed by a series of internal clocks, each running on a different schedule. The heart beats 140 times a minute, while the timer controlling sleep and awake periods in the uterus is paced very slowly, changing once every thirty minutes. The timing of these sleep and awake states changes with the age of the fetus. Most of the clocks are located in the brain; however, the pacemaker for the fetal heart is part of the heart itself. These many clocks work simultaneously and produce overlapping rhythms in the fetus. A Swiss watchmaker would never get any sleep if he had to keep all these differently timed clocks in good running order! Babies have their own characteristic time tables and rhythms when born, and a perceptive mother will notice clues about these during pregnancy.

These images show a furrowing of the brow in this thirty-two-week-old fetus. Is this a grimace or a frown?

A fetus opening its mouth

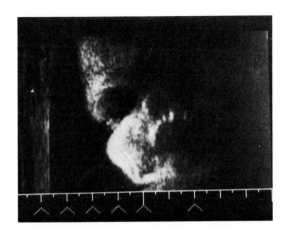 

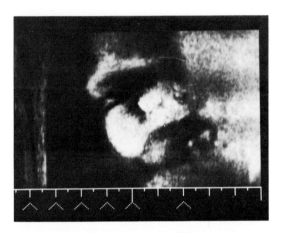 

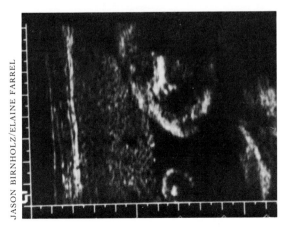 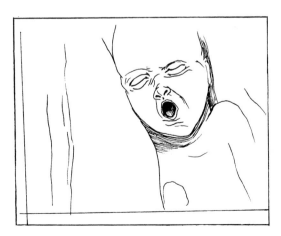

133

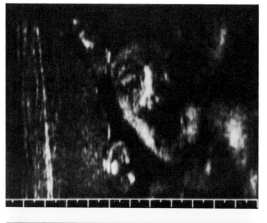

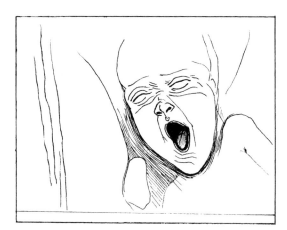

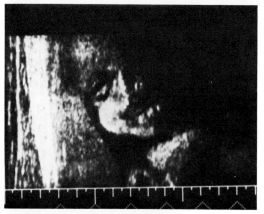

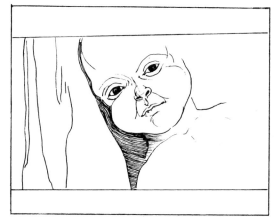

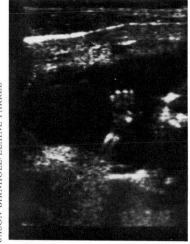

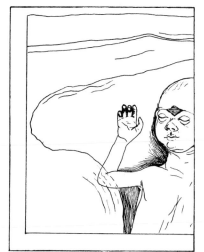

JASON BIRNHOLZ/ELAINE FARREL

134

Is this a yawn?

This fetus has an eye open. What does it see?

Could this fourteen-week-old fetus be waving to us?

The fetus is also bathed in sound. From the earliest period of pregnancy, the environment of the womb is a symphony of sounds and vibrations. Minute microphones placed alongside the fetus at six to seven months have revealed that the maternal sounds have a volume slightly less than that of a busy city street! Swishing of the blood in the mother's large blood vessels, her heartbeat, and her intestinal rumblings make up many of the sounds.

In varying degrees, the fetus is sensitive to external noises as well. Japanese researchers have made a fascinating observation while studying newborns living in the vicinity of Osaka airport, one of the world's busiest. If a pregnant woman moves into the housing near the runway before six and a half months' gestation, her three-day-old newborn will wake up only 5 percent of the time when a jet takes off. But if a woman moves into the same area after seven months of gestation, her three-day-old newborn will wake up and cry 55 percent of the time at the same occurrence. Similar experiments with buzzers have shown this same ability to "tune out," or "habituate," as researchers call it. Such an ability shows a highly sophisticated level of development in the fetus.

Further evidence of fetal hearing comes from observing the fetus through ultrasound while it is responding to clicking sounds from outside the mother's abdomen. At twenty-eight weeks, an external clicking sound produces an immediate response of the eye. Eye blinks begin in some fetuses as early as twenty-six weeks, and all healthy babies blink by twenty-eight weeks. Researchers cannot yet tell how much of this blinking comes from the actual hearing of the click and how much is related to picking up the vibrations of the click with other sense organs. However, brain waves of very young prematures do show a definite response to pure sound as early as twenty-seven weeks. If you are ever concerned that your unborn baby is too quiet and not moving, try placing a small transistor radio on your abdomen and playing some music. You will immediately know all is well when it responds to the music by moving. As we saw in Chapter 3, the fetus, while living in the uterus, develops a special interest in listening to its mother's voice.

Other senses are also well developed long before delivery. Some of the taste receptors are in use between twenty-eight and thirty weeks. Young premature infants will suck with extra vigor when given something sweet and make a face or grimace when given anything tart.

The sense of touch appears very early. There are many responses to touch that, in part, probably explain many of the movements you feel. When the soles of the feet are touched, the fetus will straighten its legs; and when its fingers come to its lips, it will suck on them. As early as six to eight weeks, if a fetus's hand or foot accidentally touches something in utero, the fingers or toes will curl; and by six months, the hand grasp is strong enough to actually support the fetus's own weight.

The fetus is also sensitive to light while in the womb and develops the capability of sight several months before the pregnancy is complete. When a bright light is flashed on and off on the mother's abdomen, a blink can be seen on ultra-sound, but it occurs with a definite delay of one second compared to the immediate blink in response to sound. Very young prematures are sometimes born with their eyelids still fused. However, they do make a blinking motion at the flash of a

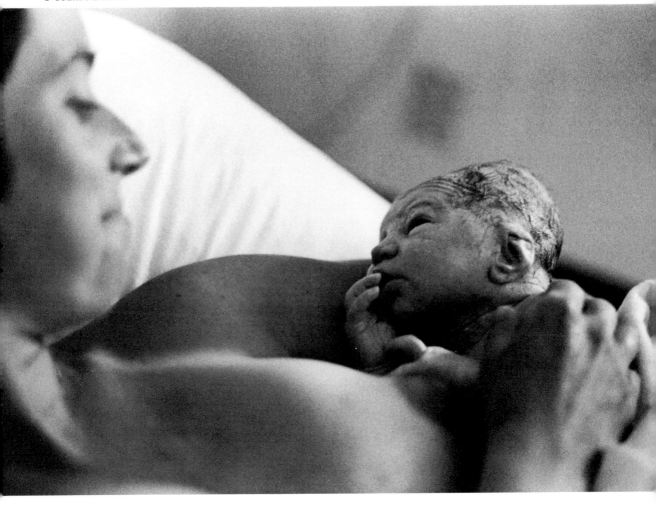

**The dialogue between mother
and baby begins.**

bright light. Light can be transmitted through the thin wall of the uterus and abdominal wall of the mother, and so the fetus probably experiences night and day. Some premature babies who have spent only thirty to thirty-one weeks in the uterus have visual preferences. When premature infants are shown thick and thin stripes, they demonstrate that they prefer to look mainly at thick stripes. These preferences keep changing, and by thirty-five to thirty-six weeks, they like to look at different kinds of shapes.

The observations of pregnant women add continually to those of researchers. The fetus, by using its newly developing senses, picks up many internal and external signals. In addition, pregnant women report that the fetus responds by a change of activity to their emotions. Obstetricians have also observed that women with chronic stress will have fetuses who have fast heart rates and are very active. By some complicated process, the fetus can be affected by its mother's emotional experiences. Consequently, the mother and her baby are engaged in a dialogue long before the baby's birth. Her activity level and emotional state interlock with the unborn baby's characteristic cycles. As she adjusts to the rhythms of this new life within her, the fetus is already experiencing the tempo of her life as well as that of its father and other members of its family.

About the Authors

Marshall H. Klaus, M.D., is professor and chairman of the Department of Pediatrics and Human Development at Michigan State University. A distinguished neonatologist, he is the author of more than one hundred scholarly papers and of several fundamental works in the field, including *Care of the High-Risk Neonate* and *Parent-Infant Bonding,* both published throughout the world. His films, including *The Amazing Newborn* and *The Ties that Bind,* are shown in maternity hospitals and prenatal classes all around the country.

Phyllis H. Klaus, M.Ed., C.S.W., is a psychotherapist, social worker, and educator. She maintains a psychotherapy practice working with families, individuals, and groups in both clinical and hospital settings. She also writes, consults, and conducts workshops throughout the country and abroad.

References

•

CHAPTER ONE

Anders, T. F.: Biological rhythms in development, *Psychosom. Med.* 44(1): 61–72, 1982.

Emde, R. N.; Swedburg, J.; and Suzuki, B.: Human wakefulness and biological rhythms after birth, *Arch. Gen. Psychiatry* 32:780–783, 1975.

Parmelee, A. H., Jr., et al.: Sleep states in premature infants, *Dev. Med. Child Neurol.* 9:70, 1967.

Prechtl, H. F. R., and Beintema, D.: Neurological examination of the full-term and newborn infant, *Clin. Dev. Med.* (London) 12, William Heineman, 1964.

Wolff, P. H.: Observation on newborn infants, *Psychosom. Med.* 21:110–118, 1959.

———: *The Causes, Controls and Organization of Behavior in the Neonate*, New York: International Universities Press, Inc., 1965.

CHAPTER TWO

Brazelton, T. B.; School, M. Z.; and Robey, J. S.: Visual responses in the newborn, *Pediatrics* 37:284–290, 1966.

Fantz, R. L.: The origin of form perception, *Sci. Am.* 204:66–72, 1961.

———: Pattern vision in newborn infants, *Science 140:296–297, 1963.*

———: Visual experience in infants: Decreased attention to familiar relative to novel ones, *Science* 146:668–670, 1964.

Goren, C.; Sarty, M.; and Wu, P.: Visual following and pattern discrimination of facelike stimuli by newborn infants, *Pediatrics* 56:544–549, 1975.

Haith, M. M.; Bergman, T.; and Moore, M. J.: Eye contact and face scanning in early infancy, *Science* 198:853–855, 1977.

CHAPTER THREE

Bower, T. G. R.: Repetitive processes in child development, *Sci. Am.* 235(5):38–47, 1976.

———: *The Perceptual World of the Child*, Cambridge: Harvard University Press, 1977.

Carpenter, G.: Mother's face and the newborn, *New Scientist* 21: 742–744, 1974.

DeCasper, A. J., and Fifer, W. P.: Of human bonding: Newborns prefer their mothers' voices, *Science* 208:1174–1176, 1980.

DeCasper, A. J., and Prescott, P. A.: Human newborns' perception of male voices: Preference, discrimination, and reinforcing value, *Dev. Psychobiol.* 17(5): 481–491, 1984.

Lipsitt, L. P.: The study of sensory and learning processes of the newborn, *Clin. Perinatology* 4(1): 163–186, 1977.

Macfarlane, A.: Olfaction in the development of social preferences in the human neonate. In *CIBA Foundation Symposium, #33*: Parent-Infant Interaction, New York: Associated Scientific Publishers, Inc., 1975.

Meltzoff, A. N., and Borton, R. W.: Intermodal matching by human neonates, *Nature* 282:403–404, 1979.

CHAPTER FOUR

Amiel-Tison, L., and Grenier, A.: *Neurologic Evaluation of the Newborn and the Infant*, New York: Masson Publishing USA, 1983.

Condon, W. S., and Sander, L. W.: Neonate movement is synchronized with adult speech: Interactional participation and language acquisition, *Science* 183:99–101, 1974.

Robertson, S. S.: Intrinsic temporal patterning in the spontaneous movement of awake neonates, *Child Dev.* 53:1016–1021, 1982.

Robertson, S. S.; Dierker, L. J.; Sorokin, Y.; and Rosen, M. G.: Human fetal movement: Spontaneous oscillations near one cycle per minute, *Science* 218:1327–1330, 1982.

CHAPTER FIVE

Ekman, P., and Oster, H.: Facial expressions of emotion, *Ann. Rev. Psychol.* 30:527–554, 1979.

Field, T. M.; Woodson, R.; Greenberg, R.; and Cohen, D.: Discrimination and imitation of facial expressions by neonates, *Science* 218:179–181, 1982.

Maratos, O.: Trends in the development of imitation in early infancy. In Bever, T. G., ed., *Regressions in Mental Development*, Hillsdale, N.J.: Lawrence Eribsum Assoc., 1982.

Meltzoff, A. N., and Moore, M. K.: Imitation of facial and manual gestures by human neonates, *Science* 198:75–78, 1977.

Meltzoff, A. N., and Moore, M. K.: Newborn infants imitate adult facial gestures, *Child Dev.* 54:702–709, 1983.

Winnicott, D. W.: *Playing and Reality*, London: Tavistock Publications, Ltd., 1971.

CHAPTER SIX

Brazelton, T. B.: *Infants and Mothers*, Revised Edition, New York: Delacorte Press/Lawrence, 1983.

Kennell, J. H., and Klaus, M. H.: Care of the mother of the high-risk infant, *Clin. Obst. Gyn.* 14:926–954, 1971.

Klaus, M. H., and Kennell, J. H.: *Parent-Infant Bonding*, St. Louis: C. V. Mosby Co., 1982.

Macfarlane, A.; Smith, D. M.; and Garrow, D. H.: The relationship between mother and neonate; in Kitzinger, S., and Davis, J. A., editors: *The Place of Birth*, New York: Oxford University Press, 1978.

Parke, R. D.: Perspectives on father-infant interactions; in Osofsky, J. D., editor: *The Handbook of Infant Development*, New York: John Wiley & Sons, Inc., 1979.

Robertson, J., and Robertson, J.: Young children in brief separation: A fresh look, *Psychoanalytic Study of the Child* 26:264–315, 1971.

Rodholm, M., and Larsson, K.: Father-infant interaction at the first contact after delivery, *Early Hum. Dev.* 3:21–27, 1979.

Stern, D.: *The First Relationship: Infant and Mother*, Cambridge: Harvard University Press, 1974.

Winnicott, D. W.: *The Child, the Family, and the Outside World*, New York: Penguin Books, 1964.

———: *Through Pediatrics to Psycho-Analysis*, New York: Basic Books, Inc., 1958.

CHAPTER SEVEN

Ando, Y., and Hattori, H.: Effects of noise on sleep on babies, *J. Acoust. Soc. Am.* 62(1): 199–204, 1977.

Birnholz, J. C., and Benacerraf, B. R.: The development of human fetal hearing, *Science* 222:516–518, 1983.

Birnholz, J. C., and Farrell, E. E.: Ultrasound images of human fetal development, *Am. Sci.* 72:608–614, 1984.

Macfarlane, A.: *The Psychology of Childbirth*, Cambridge: Harvard University Press, 1977.

Index